Diary of a
CAT

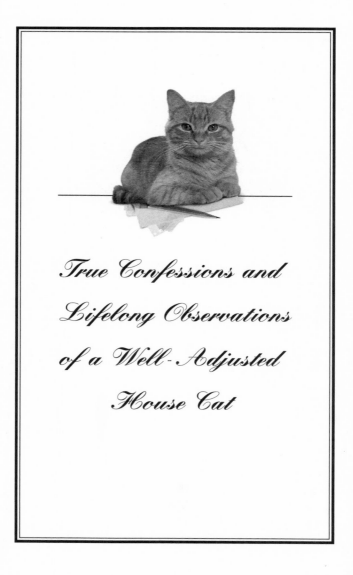

True Confessions and

Lifelong Observations

of a Well-Adjusted

House Cat

Diary of a CAT

LEIGH W. RUTLEDGE

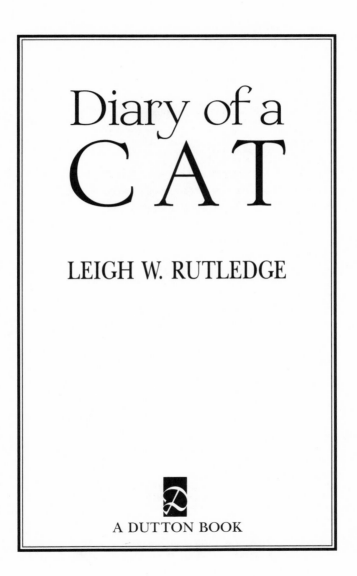

A DUTTON BOOK

DUTTON
Published by the Penguin Group
Penguin Books USA Inc., 375 Hudson Street,
New York, New York 10014, U.S.A.
Penguin Books Ltd, 27 Wrights Lane, London W8 5TZ, England
Penguin Books Australia Ltd, Ringwood, Victoria, Australia
Penguin Books Canada Ltd, 10 Alcorn Avenue, Toronto,
Ontario, Canada M4V 3B2
Penguin Books (N.Z.) Ltd, 182–190 Wairau Road, Auckland 10, New Zealand

Penguin Books Ltd, Registered Offices: Harmondsworth, Middlesex, England

First published by Dutton, an imprint of Dutton Signet,
a division of Penguin Books USA Inc.
Distributed in Canada by McClelland & Stewart Inc.

First Printing, November, 1995
10 9 8 7 6 5 4 3 2 1

LIBRARY OF CONGRESS CATALOGING-IN-PUBLICATION DATA
Rutledge, Leigh W.
    Diary of a cat : true confessions and lifelong observations of a
well-adjusted house cat / Leigh W. Rutledge.
       p.   cm.
    ISBN 0-525-94003-0
    1. Cats—Humor.   I. Title.
PN6162.R88   1995
818'.5407—dc20   95-21791
                                                           CIP

Printed in the United States of America
Set in Baskerville
Designed by Eve L. Kirch

PUBLISHER'S NOTE
This is a work of fiction. Names, characters, places, and incidents either are
the products of the author's imagination or are used fictitiously, and any re-
semblance to actual persons, living or dead, events, or locales is entirely
coincidental.

*To my parents, who—I've realized
as I've gotten older—planted
most of the seeds.*

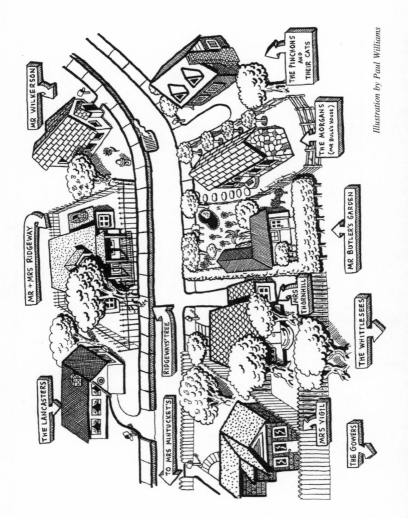

MR WILKERSON

THE PINCHONS AND THEIR CATS

THE MORGANS (MR BULL'S HOUSE)

MR BUTLER'S GARDEN

MR + MRS RIDGEWAY

MRS THORNHILL

THE WHITTLESEES

RIDGEWAY'S TREE

THE LANCASTERS

TO MRS MINTUCKET'S

MRS VIGIL

THE GOWERS

Illustration by Paul Williams

SUMMER

June 25

Slept.

June 26

Slept.

Climbed the walls today. Mrs. Vigil got new wall-paper in the bathroom. Flocked. Nothing quite like it. Like sinking my claws into plush mouse fur.

Traveled around the neighborhood this evening. Made a quick escape while Mrs. V was bringing groceries into the house. I raced out between her ankles, and she lost her balance and dumped rolls of toilet paper all over the front porch. "That stupid cat . . ." she hissed, and slammed the door. A minute later—prompted by guilt, no doubt—she was outside again, calling my name and making kissy noises. I watched every detail of her exasperation from under the junipers. She finally washed her hands of me and shut the door.

The streets were full of children and couples, people strolling in the warm evening air. As soon as I was on the street, a little boy on a tricycle started pedaling maniacally toward me. By the time I leapt out of his way, it was too late for him—his tricycle banged into the curb, and he started wailing loudly.

Mrs. Thornhill next door was having an argument in the front yard with her teenage daughter.

"You are *not* psychic," Mrs. T hollered as she yanked dandelions from the lawn.

"But I *am* psychic," her daughter cried, "and there's nothing you can do about it."

"Just because someone calls you on the telephone when you're thinking about them does *not* mean you're psychic," Mrs. T moaned. "It happens all the time to *everybody*."

"You're just jealous," her daughter shouted, "because I'm psychic and you're not!"

Sat for a long time in Mr. Butler's flower bed. Watched bugs, smelled the marigolds and delphiniums. A big, blue dragonfly started to land on my nose, then realized I wasn't a rock. I was too sleepy to chase after him. I finally went home around twilight.

Mrs. V peeked through the curtains just as I was trotting up the front steps. She swooped out in her big red kimono and gathered me in her arms as if I'd been gone for days. "Oh, it's time to come in," she cried. I could tell she'd been sitting in her armchair and fretting.

She gave me a nice bowl of milk, and the two of us later fell asleep together in front of the television.

Two fur balls today.

Aunt Petra is here visiting from Cleveland. She's Mrs. V's sister. Two minutes into the house and she clunked toward me, her big arms stretched wide. I ran under the sofa where she couldn't reach me. "Oh, why does kitty run from me?" she cooed unhappily. Why, indeed . . . Her breath smells of toothpaste, pastrami, and vodka. Haven't people ever watched how two cats greet each other? With a gentle series of *sniffs*? Cats always touch noses before initiating any kind of relationship. But people will breathe right in your face and make your eyes burn when they grab you. *In*halation, not *ex*halation—that's the key to a cat's heart.

From under the sofa, I could see Auntie's plump ankles. She was waiting impatiently for me to come out. The usual tricks were tried: the plastic ball, the kitty treat, the old sock waved back and forth in front of my face. She walked to the left, then to the right, then scouted around the back of the sofa as if looking for a strategic way to get at me. After several minutes she finally gave up, and I could hear her complain to Mrs. V, "You have the *strangest* cat . . ."

Odd, how disheartened people usually feel when they're rejected by an animal; they seem to have staked a good deal of their self-esteem on how animals, children, cards, and the stock market react to them.

Stuck under the sofa hiding from her much of the afternoon.

Slept on top of the car today. Hissed at one of the neighborhood dogs. Slept on top of the car some more.

Mrs. Mintucket was out for a walk. She lives a block away, is in her seventies, and it's said she hasn't been out of her house in almost twenty years. Recently, she's been trying to expand her frontiers. Unfortunately, she was at a dead stop right in front of our house. She was trying to persuade her feet to go the length of just one more concrete block in the sidewalk; but while her ambition was strong, her legs were unwilling. "Just a little bit farther," she said to her shoes, as if they were terrified children. "Just a few more steps, and then we'll go home." She waited, and stared down for a moment. But her shoes wouldn't respond. "Listen," she finally snapped, "do you think I'm going to spend what little time I have left staring at the same old neighborhood, the same old houses, the same old street?! I've got places to go, things I want to see before I die!" Her shoes wouldn't budge. She finally sighed in resignation and turned around. "Maybe tomorrow . . ." she said and shuffled toward home.

Spent most of the day, as always on the Fourth of July, locked in the laundry room. Mrs. V snatched me from a cozy nap on top of the television. "You belong in the laundry room today," she told me, gently stroking my head but holding my front paws tight. "And besides," she whispered in my ear, "Aunt Petra won't find you there."

Once incarcerated, I perched myself in the window and watched two squirrels chase each other round and round a tree trunk outside. I envied their freedom—squirrels don't have to answer to anybody for anything. I planted myself on a pair of panty hose that had been left on top of the dryer; I tried kneading them first to make them a little comfier. They weren't quite right, so I had to get up and knead them some more.

Fell quickly asleep—only to be awakened by Aunt Petra clutching me to her breasts and hissing triumphantly, "I've got you now, you wicked little thing." Her breath smelled of watermelon and beer.

"Now, why does kitty always run from me?" she asked, twisting one of my ears, yanking on my whiskers, and accidentally poking me in the eye with a finger.

It's never so much me she takes pleasure in as it is the *conquest* of me; but then, that's the way it is with most people.

Fireworks tonight. I watched from the window and remembered how, when I was a kitten, they fascinated me so much I sometimes leapt against the glass at them.

July 5

Played with a catnip mouse. Knocked my head into a dining-room table leg. Slept.

It is my birthday today. But no one noticed. The birthdays of cats are like the obituaries of strangers—people just skip right over them. I am three years old.

I often wonder what became of my mother. Did anyone ever take her in? Did she ever find a fireplace and a food dish of her own? Whenever I think of her, I see a skinny, young alley cat old before her time. Her fur was orange and gray, and her eyes were emerald green. Her trilling was melodic, and whenever she called, all five of us immediately came running—we could hear her voice, anxious and beautiful, from far away. I remember how safe I felt with my nose buried in her belly. She smelled of mustard weed and dust. Where is she now? What, I wonder, is she doing at this exact moment? I'll never know.

She was a good mother.

It isn't true that cats aren't sentimental—it just looks that way sometimes because we're so experienced at accepting the inevitable. Separation, flea baths, distemper shots—it all happens whether you want it to or not.

Weather hot and sticky. Even the linoleum in the kitchen didn't feel cool.

Aunt Petra left to go home to Cleveland this morning. "Oh, isn't kitty going to give me a good-bye kiss?" she warbled. She was serious. Feeling in an unusually generous mood, I let her stroke my back. She seized the opportunity to plant a big red lipstick mark on my forehead. "You have the *sweetest* cat," she told Mrs. V.

I watched her leave and thought, If you were a bird, I'd eat you . . .

The afternoon was spent in quiet contemplation on the front lawn. Mrs. V trimmed her roses; I sat in the grass. A nice breeze rustled through the trees overhead. Mrs. V was very quiet. She sighed as she clipped the deadwood off the rose bushes. After a while, she joined me on the grass.

"Oh, I know Petra's a nuisance sometimes," she told me, gently stroking my fur. "She drinks too much. And she cheats at canasta. But I hate it every time she leaves. Isn't it stupid?" After a moment, she picked me up and held me very close with her face buried in the back of my neck.

"I hate growing old," she whispered.

Bored. Knocked stuff off the kitchen counter. Same old stuff, same old kitchen counter. It all bounces on the floor the same way whether you swat it, flick it, nudge it, or sweep it off with your tail. The vitamin bottles always make a nice sound when they crash, though.

Fell asleep by the water dish.

Mrs. V and I watched *Out of Africa* on TV tonight. During the commercials she kept scratching my fur in a rambunctious manner and murmured, "Oh, you're my little tiger, aren't you? I bet you wish *you* were out there chasing antelope and water buffalo, don't you? Oh, my little tiger, my little tiger . . ."

She's promised to rent *The Birds* for the weekend.

Terrible fight between Mrs. Thornhill and her daughter this morning. I was sitting in the grass admiring a plump grasshopper on the rose trellis when the two of them came charging out their front door. The grasshopper panicked at all the noise and disappeared headfirst into the ivy.

"You're not bringing him to *my* family reunion," Mrs. T hollered, chasing her daughter onto the lawn.

"I'm eighteen, and I'll do as I please! It's my family, too, you know!" her daughter screamed.

"You're not going to ruin the reunion just to prove a point . . ."

"We're going to be married next summer, Mother. I *love* him. And he loves *me*."

"Then why does he make you wear a *beeper*?!" Mrs. T bellowed.

There was a stunned silence, as if the daughter had been caught off guard. "He just likes to know where I am," her daughter replied defensively.

Mrs. T grunted in disbelief. "I'm surprised he doesn't make you wear a collar with a little bell on it," she said disgustedly.

"You're just jealous," her daughter shouted,

"because I have a man and you don't anymore!"

She disappeared back into the house and slammed the front door so hard that grasshoppers all around me leapt up from their hiding places.

Why do people argue about everything except what's important? The Lancasters across the street have a running argument over who's going to mow the lawn each weekend. Every Saturday, Mr. and Mrs. Gower (they live behind us) get into an argument over the best way to light the barbecue. There are people who drive by the house—I don't even know who they are—who shout at one another as they speed down the road.

Cats only argue about important things: food, a warm place to nap, and, once or twice a year, sex.

Mrs. Thornhill was sitting on her front steps mumbling to herself, so I wandered over and said hello. When she saw me, she stretched out her hand and called, "Kitty, kitty . . . Here, kitty, kitty . . ."

I wound my way toward her and brushed against her legs.

"You know," she said, scratching my ear, "sometimes I wish she'd just move out and never come back. I sometimes think we'd be better off if we never had anything to do with each other again. Why does she hate me so much? When she was a little girl, she *worshiped* me. *Now* look at her . . ."

From inside the house, I could hear the daughter yelling, "I *hate* this house! I *hate* this town! I hate everyone and *everything*!"

Mrs. T sighed, frisked my chin, and then said, with such good-natured affection I didn't take offense, "Stupid cat—you never have to worry about *anything*."

New litter box today. Nice shade of blue. Bigger than the old one. Very luxurious. Sat in it for an hour just to enjoy the feel of it. Noticed a weird speck of dirt that didn't belong in the litter. Tried to get it out. Dug and dug, hurled litter every which way. Lost sight of the speck, so I started flinging litter straight up in the air to see if I could find it again. Gave up—never did get the speck out. Went to play in the garden.

Under the weather. Sniffles, tired, felt all day like a giant fur ball was coming up at any moment. It never did, though. Like having a hairy grapefruit stuck in one's throat. I didn't complain—until they come up with a new way to take cats' temperatures, most of us will downplay our ailments.

In the afternoon I slept, dreaming of mice the size of armadillos, and of chasing them through open fields and bringing them home for dinner.

After I woke up, I got a glimpse of myself in the living-room mirror. Am I really that small? I wondered with a jolt.

In my dreams I'd been as big as a lion.

Mr. Bull is my best friend. He lives with the Morgans, three houses down. They call him Mr. Bull because he pushes his head into everything: he climbs up onto people's chests and pushes his head into their faces when he wants affection, he pushes his head into the furniture when there are no faces available, he even pushes his head into the rear end of the Morgans' dog, Ralph. This makes Ralph jump, and he sometimes turns and gives Mr. Bull a little growl, but most of the time he just looks confused and vaguely panic-stricken as if he knows he's dealing with an unpredictable clown.

Mr. Bull and I spend a lot of time digging through people's trash, exploring everyone's yards, and playing with bugs. This afternoon we snuck into the Whittlesees' backyard to stare at their dog, Spook. Spook has so much hair in his eyes he's constantly bumping into things and getting lost in his own backyard. This provides Mr. Bull and me with considerable amusement.

As we were sitting on the fence waiting for Spook to come out, there was an awful racket from one of the Whittlesees' open windows. "You listen to me, you rotten little jerk," Mr. Whittlesee was shouting. "You ever do that again, and I'll *kill* you. Do you understand? I'll kill you!" We could hear a little boy crying, and then the sound of several hard smacks being delivered, and then Mr. Whittlesee yelling again, "Go to your room now before I really give you something to cry about!"

Mr. Bull and I jumped back over the fence and sat for a long time, very quietly, in Mr. Butler's garden.

Got one of my claws caught in the sofa this morning. I was scratching one of the cushions, when I suddenly realized I was stuck. I twisted to the left; I twisted to the right. I yanked and yanked. Nothing happened. I finally had to sit for twenty minutes until Mrs. V came into the room and noticed me moored to the furniture.

"Serves you right for scratching my couch," she said, detaching my claw from the fabric.

I gave her my best dejected look.

"You like to think you're so independent," she said, walking away, "but the fact is you'd be very unhappy on your own."

Mrs. Mintucket was out again this afternoon. She made it all the way down to Mr. Butler's garden. But then she lost her nerve and turned around. As she passed by our house on her way home, she was arguing with her shoes again.

"If *you* won't take me where I want to go," she warned them, "I'll find a pair of shoes that *will*!"

Her shoes, as usual, had nothing to say.

"Look what I brought *you* today!" Mrs. V announced this morning, after she'd been out shopping. She plopped a fat gray kitten on the carpet in front of me. "Oh, it was *terrible*," she said, her voice quivering. "I was driving down Sunny Vale Road, when the car in front of me suddenly pulled to a stop, and I saw them throw *this* out of the window. Can you *imagine?* What's wrong with people these days?"

The kitten and I stared at each other. It had a happy, vacant look on its face. I hissed, hit it once on the head, and ran under the sofa.

"I don't know if we're going to keep it," Mrs. V said at first.

But by evening she'd named it "Bobbie Boop." A tremor of disgust went through me. "Yes," she proclaimed, picking him up and shaking him excitedly. "Bobbie Boop, Bobbie Boop . . ."

This evening, Bobbie Boop was lying on his back in the bathroom sink with all four legs sticking up in the air.

I would have given anything to turn the faucet on.

The Pinchons down the street have twenty-three house cats, but you never see any of the cats outside enjoying themselves. Instead, you sometimes see them in the windows, staring out with a plaintive expression on their faces. They look like immigrants on an overcrowded ship.

The Pinchons have been collecting cats for a long time. Mr. Pinchon is a banker, a short, bald, good-natured man; you can sometimes see him through the windows holding a cat in the air like a newborn baby and rubbing noses with it. Mrs. Pinchon is rather thin and dark and anxious, with restless hands and frenzied eyes— the kind of person you always suspect is up to something. She's constantly on the lookout for more animals.

If an unfamiliar cat strays into her yard, she's outside in an instant. "Oh, who are *you*?" she demands. "Do you have a home? Oh, you poor, *poor* thing . . ." It doesn't matter if the cat is half dead or as plump as a Sunday roast; she addresses each one as "a poor, poor thing" and wrings her hands in a greedy gesture of despair. She did this to me once, but I just walked away. "Wait! Come back!"

she called after me. "I'll give you a good home. I have *catnip* inside."

I'm not sure why I've been thinking about the Pinchons all day. I think of them every time I look at Bobbie Boop. One cat is fine, but once a person gets two they sometimes start thinking to themselves, "Well, two isn't so bad. How much more trouble can *three* be . . ." Next thing you know, there's never any room on the bed anymore, all the good heating ducts are taken in the winter, and you have to wait in line to use the litter box.

An awful lot of otherwise sane people wind up like the Pinchons.

Terrible thunderstorm today. It caught me off guard while I was out playing. I waited it out under a stack of firewood in the Whittlesees' backyard. I wasn't alone. The Whittlesees' young son (he must be ten or eleven) was sitting out back in the rain. He just sat there, on a picnic bench, getting drenched. He had an unhappy expression on his face, and he was biting his nails.

"Now," Mrs. V said this afternoon, "I want you to teach Bobbie Boop everything you know about life."

She set the two of us out on the front lawn and then disappeared inside—but I could see her peeking through the front drapes.

Bobbie Boop sat in the grass and watched gnats buzz around his ears. His head went round and round until his eyes were crossed. I tried to ignore him, but there was a hard tap on the front window, and I could see Mrs. V emphatically mouthing the words, "Show him the yard . . ."

So reluctantly I showed him the rose trellis, where all the best grasshoppers sit, and I showed him where to duck under the porch when dogs come by. I showed him which are the best flowers to lie in and which spiders he should stay away from. After a while, he stopped listening and started chasing himself in circles. Once, he bit his tail so hard it made him jump three feet, and he looked confused as if trying to figure out, Who did that? Kittens can be pitifully stupid.

All of a sudden, a big white butterfly—its wings were so wide and heavy it flapped them slowly, like some great bird—swooped to a landing in the middle of the lawn. It folded its giant wings behind it and stared at us with black, defiant eyes while gently nibbling on something in the grass.

Neither one of us moved. We were awestruck.

The butterfly gave us an insolent look, as if daring us to pounce, and then effortlessly lifted itself back in the air. It came soaring right over Bobbie Boop's head (I could see the tiny hairs on his ears flutter), and then rose up into the sky until its whiteness was lost against the clouds.

We didn't budge, and Bobbie Boop stared at the sky for a long time, with a look of indescribable yearning on his face. He looked for a moment as if he might take flight himself and follow the butterfly into the clouds.

Played solitaire tonight with Mrs. V and Bobbie Boop. At one point Bobbie Boop jumped on the ace of hearts and went sailing right over the edge of the card table.

Sat in the grass today; thought about dinner. When the sun got too hot, I moved to another part of the yard and thought about dinner some more.

Two women walked by and stared at me.

"What do you suppose cats think about all the time?" one asked the other.

"Oh, nothing at all," said her companion. "I don't think they think about much of anything. They're not very smart."

"But, what if they are?" insisted the one. "What if they're sitting around all day contemplating a cure for cancer or thinking about nuclear fusion? What if they're in contact with extraterrestrials and refuse to tell us about it? What if they've discovered the meaning of life? What if they know something we don't?"

"My dear," the other said, laughing gaily, "if they were that smart, *they'd* be in control, not us . . ."

At that instant, an old suitcase full of dolls came flying out the Thornhills' front door and landed on the sidewalk with a crash. The front door slammed shut, and there was no sign of anyone.

One little doll lay on its back, like the victim of a plane crash, in Mrs. Thornhill's iris bed, and the head of another went rolling down the gutter. A tiny blue bonnet swayed from the lilacs.

The two women stared down at the broken suitcase, looked up at the Thornhills' house, then started walking again.

"She certainly has her hands full these days, doesn't she?" said the one.

"Yes," said the other, with a sigh. "I often wonder if children shouldn't all be shipped off to a desert island until they're twenty-one."

Rained all day. I couldn't go out. Mrs. V wrote letters. I went to help her. "It's hard enough writing letters," she finally told me in exasperation, "without you playing with the pen." She tossed me on the carpet. I made her do it three times before conceding the point. Then I started gnawing on her chair leg. "Go away, go, go," she insisted. "Surely, you have something better to do with your time . . ."

I trotted into the living room and sat for a long time watching Bobbie Boop asleep on the sofa. He's actually grown in the two weeks since we got him. I have to admit, his ridiculous face, with its big eyes and those long, gray hairs sticking out of his ears, has started to grow on me.

Then it suddenly occurred to me: I'm old enough to be his father—I'm not a kitten anymore. That disturbed me, because some part of me still thinks of myself as a kitten, as a playful, silly, unpredictable kitten.

All at once, I felt *old*.

I never knew my own father. Never even got a glimpse of him, not once, though sometimes I see a reflection of my face in a hubcap or the patio door, and I think to myself that there must be some part of him in there somewhere. He ran off before we were born. And really, we never missed him. Our mother took care of everything: she fed us, she taught us to hunt, she taught us to hide, she played with us and never complained once, even when all five of us would pounce on her at the same time.

I must remember to ask Mr. Bull if he knew his father. I doubt it. Cats are by nature a fatherless species.

The sun broke through the clouds this morning, and long before Mrs. V was dressed I was pawing at the windows, eager to go out. Once outside, Bobbie Boop and I danced through the grass, and chased each other around the lilacs, and at one point we rolled together, playfully wrestling, across the front porch. Even Mrs. V, when she finally joined us, seemed to be doing a little jig as she walked around the garden checking her flowers.

The three of us watched *2001* tonight. Bobbie Boop dozed off halfway through.

When the movie was finished, Mrs. V sat very quietly for several minutes with me in her lap. She got up, carrying me in her arms, and went to the window. "What do you suppose is *really* out there?" she asked, looking up at the sky. "What do you suppose it's *really* like?" She took a deep breath and sighed. "Sometimes I wish I could live forever just so I could see it all . . ."

Bobbie Boop was missing this morning. He wasn't on the sofa. He wasn't under the bed. He wasn't in the bathroom sink. Mrs. V looked through all the closets and behind the living-room furniture. She went outside and called his name a dozen times.

She decided to check the bathroom and the kitchen a second time. She opened all the cabinets to see if he was trapped.

She finally found him among the pots and pans under the stove. He was curled up in a big soup pot.

"Oh, how convenient," she joked. "We won't even have to move him to cook him for dinner."

He stared up at her with sleepy eyes.

"An idle Boop is the Devil's workshop," she warned as she fished him out of the pot.

Tonight she secured the kitchen cabinets so he can't get into them anymore.

Big bird on the maple tree in the front yard this morning. I sat and watched it through the living-room window for ten minutes. I was so desperate to get at it I got entangled in the mini-blinds and brought them all down on my head.

Bobbie Boop looked at me as if to say, Some role model you are.

Delightful weather. Fence-walking weather. Warm and sunny and dry.

Mrs. Thornhill's daughter was out sunbathing on the back lawn. She was complaining about her mother to someone on the telephone. "She's just jealous," she hollered, "because she's all middle-aged now and I still have my whole life ahead of me . . ."

Mrs. Morgan was hanging plastic pineapples and Chinese lanterns from her trees; she's having a party tonight. She was singing to herself while Mr. Bull rolled around on the ground, trying to eat her shoelaces.

When I went by the Pinchons' house, I noticed Mrs. Pinchon dozing in a crouched position under her back steps. Her hands were loosely holding one end of a very long string; the other end was tied to a small hot dog on the sidewalk. She'd obviously been hoping for a stray cat to come by.

Spied on the Whittlesee boy while he was playing in his backyard. He's a skinny boy with big brown eyes and hair as black as a black cat.

He was bouncing a tennis ball on the patio and talking to himself. I couldn't hear what he was saying, but he was obviously having a very enthusiastic conversation.

He suddenly spotted a spider on the patio and stood over it for a moment. I thought to myself: Here it comes—he's going to squish it. People love to kill things . . .

Instead, he leaned over, smiled, and said, "Hello, Mr. Spider. Are you having a good day? I hope you're having a good day."

Then he moved to a different part of the patio as if to make certain he didn't hurt it with his ball.

After a while, he sat on the lawn and pulled strands of grass out of the ground and held them up with a quizzical expression to the sunlight. Then he curled up and fell asleep.

I sat in the grass a few feet away and watched him sleep—and thought how it sometimes seems as if people are all just barely holding on to a moment's contentment.

Went home for an early dinner.

AUTUMN

Unraveled all the toilet paper this afternoon.

I didn't mean to undo the whole roll, but once I got started I couldn't help myself.

"Good grief," Mrs. V moaned as she stood in the doorway. "What have you done?"

I blinked at her from underneath the pile I'd created. When she tried to pick up a piece, I snatched it back.

She looked startled.

She tried to pick up another piece.

I snatched it back as well.

"I'm *not* going to get into a war of wills with you," she announced, grabbing a long piece—which I promptly seized with my claws and yanked back.

She studied me for a moment.

"I don't like the look of your eyes at all," she said.

It was true: looking up at her, I felt as if I were peering out from some lair on the African veldt. I had an image of chasing *her* through open fields . . .

She suddenly stamped her feet back and forth, and I ran out of the room.

"Some people buy little winter jackets for *their* cats," she remarked as she went for the broom. "I need straitjackets for *mine* . . ."

Slept on the sofa all afternoon. Was awakened by a sudden noise and saw Bobbie Boop scamper by with Mrs. V's reading glasses in his mouth.

A few minutes after that, I cracked one eye open and saw him run by with a twenty-dollar bill between his teeth.

A moment later, he was dragging the toaster away by its electrical cord.

Went back to sleep.

"Where are my reading glasses?" Mrs. V demanded this evening. "I can't imagine what I've done with them . . ."

A short time after that, she went into the kitchen. "And *where's* the toaster?" she asked.

She turned and looked at Bobbie Boop and me.

"What are the two of you up to now?" she asked.

She shook her head. "I suppose you're planning to have a garage sale and use the proceeds to take a Caribbean cruise," she mused.

I glanced over at Bobbie Boop.

He had the most demure and innocent expression on his face.

"You two certainly are a mystery these days," Mrs. V said.

Up on the roof today. Nice breeze. Good view of the neighborhood. Could see Mr. Bull sound asleep in a wheelbarrow in Mrs. Thornhill's backyard. A bluejay gave me an indignant glance as it flew by.

Moved to a different part of the roof. Could see right into one of the Thornhills' bedroom windows. A commotion was going on. Mrs. T was running with a jug of water in her hands, and there was smoke coming from the bathroom. Her daughter sat laughing.

When she came out of the bathroom, Mrs. T raced to the bedroom window and flung it open.

". . . prom dress," she was saying.

"Leave me alone," her daughter sulked.

"You could've burnt the house down . . ."

"I don't care."

"Is that your response to everything these days—'I don't care'?!"

"You're just . . ."

"Stop it!" Mrs. T barked with such authority that it instantly silenced her daughter. "Don't even say it! I am *not* jealous of you."

She sighed and sat down, obviously exhausted.

Her daughter didn't move.

"Of course, I wish I were younger," Mrs. T told her. "Of course, I wish I wasn't alone. But that doesn't mean I'm jealous of you. Don't you understand I *want* to see you happy? Can't you see I'm trying to save you *years* of frustration?"

"I don't want *you* to decide what will make me happy," the daughter said imperiously.

There was a long pause.

"That's the first *adult* thing you've said to me in weeks," Mrs. T told her.

They were both silent for a long time.

"I'm sorry about the dress," her daughter said.

"At least the whole bathroom didn't go up in smoke!"

They laughed.

"When you want to get rid of old clothes," Mrs. T told her, "just *throw* them away. But you know, there may come a time when you wish you hadn't destroyed *everything* from your childhood. You'll wish you had it back someday so you could take it out to look at it just one more time . . ."

Her daughter bristled.

"I don't need any of this junk anymore," she

snapped. "I don't need to spend *my* time moon-
ing over the past."

"It isn't a matter of *need*," her mother said
wearily.

She got up and walked into another room.

Her daughter rolled her eyes, hesitated, and
then followed.

A trip to the vet's this morning. Bobbie Boop got his booster shots; I got an annual checkup.

Our vet, Dr. Bird, is a large, happy man; he looks like a walrus with glasses. "Come in, come in!" he exclaimed when he saw us in the waiting room. "How are you? And how's the new addition?" He gave Bobbie Boop several vigorous pats on the head. "Get me Mrs. Vigil's file immediately!" he told his receptionist.

The receptionist looked at us hopelessly. Her fingers were stained with ink, and she sat at a desk overrun by paperwork. There were computer printouts, appointment ledgers, and file folders everywhere. There were also stacks of mail to go out: Dr. Bird sends a personal get-well card to every animal who comes to his office.

"I'll be with you in a few minutes, Mrs. Pennymarch!" he told a woman who was sitting in the waiting room with a Lhasa Apso in her lap and a parrot on her shoulder. Every few seconds, the parrot leaned over and stole stray hairs from the top of the Lhasa Apso's head and then neatly arranged them on the woman's shoulder. I wondered if it was planning to build a nest right there.

"And how are you, Mr. Hestermann?" Dr. Bird asked a small elderly man who was sitting with six full-grown Dobermans at his feet.

"Oh, Siegfried and Gunther and Hans and Wolfgang and Hermann and Dieter and I are in no hurry today," Mr. Hestermann replied.

In the examining room there was, to our surprise, a huge, pink cockatoo sitting on a perch in the corner.

It eyed us suspiciously as we went in. "Now, don't pay any attention to Esmeralda," Dr. Bird warned us. "She's just here temporarily."

"Aaak, aaak, stupid cats, stupid cats," Esmeralda squawked.

"Now, Esmeralda," Dr. Bird told her, "we mustn't pass judgment on other species."

"Arghhhh, arghhhh, did you hear the one about the cat and the lawn mower?"

"That's enough, Esmeralda."

Bobbie Boop's shots took barely a moment. He didn't seem to mind at all. He was overwhelmed by the sight of Esmeralda, a bird at least ten times as big as he is.

"And now," Dr. Bird said, turning to me, "it's time for your examination!"

"Did you ever find a good home for Max?" Mrs. V asked as Dr. Bird peered up my nose with a flashlight.

Max was a cat who'd been hit by a car. One of his legs had had to be amputated, and when the people he lived with realized they were getting a three-legged cat back, they wanted poor Max put to sleep: the thought of having to look at a three-legged cat running around the house was too much for them. Dr. Bird tried to talk them out of it, but they had insisted. So Dr. Bird took Max into a back room, waited five minutes, and then came out and told them, "Little Max is in heaven now . . ." In fact, he'd only pretended to put him to sleep.

Dr. Bird's back rooms are full of cats and dogs and even rabbits and gerbils he's spared from unscrupulous owners.

"Oh, yes," Dr. Bird said, gently poking my abdomen. "A very good home. A wonderful home!"

"I'm so relieved," said Mrs. V. "I was almost going to take him myself."

I looked up at her.

"Don't look at me like that," she said. "I was *tempted*, that's all . . ."

"Aak, aak, the only good cat is a dead cat," Esmeralda screeched. "Dead cat, dead cat."

Bobbie Boop was stalking around to the side of Esmeralda and started leaning dangerously close to her, as if longing to get a good sniff. His tail was twitching.

"I apologize for Esmeralda," Dr. Bird told us, neatly scooping up Bobbie Boop with one hand and depositing him into Mrs. V's arms. "She's lived in a saloon all her life, and when the owner died last week no one knew what to do with her. No matter where I put her now, she insults everyone. I had her in the dog examining room, but she kept making indecent jokes about Lassie and Rin-Tin-Tin. When I had her in the waiting room, she insulted the clients."

Dr. Bird led us out of the examination room and closed the door behind him. We could hear Esmeralda still carrying on inside. "Did you hear the one about the cat and the Cuisinart? Did you hear the one about the cat and the vacuum cleaner . . ."

"We'll see you in a few weeks," Dr. Bird told us, shaking his head.

"I'll have to send the bill to you," the receptionist told Mrs. V. "I haven't been able to find our receipt book for two weeks."

Bobbie Boop was so rambunctious on the way home, he got himself tangled up in the steering wheel and nearly got us into an accident.

Mrs. Mintucket was out trying to explore the neighborhood again this afternoon. This time she had on a pair of brand-new, bright-red sneakers.

"Oh, yes, these are much better," she said as she walked briskly down the sidewalk. "Much, much better. Wait a minute. Hold on. Slow down. Slow down! Oh, my God, where are you taking me?!"

The last I saw her, she was speeding around the corner at the end of the block.

Nice, long bath today. I started with my back legs just after lunch. By midafternoon, I had worked my way up to my stomach. By sundown, between fits of dozing, I was finishing up the ears.

Cleanliness is the best revenge.

On second thought, tuna fish is the best revenge. Cleanliness is the second-best revenge.

Kitten stuck in a tree this afternoon. It happened in front of the Ridgeways' house. No one could figure out who the kitten belonged to or where it had come from.

"Someone call the fire department!" Mrs. Ridgeway cried. She's in her midsixties and is a plump, vigorous woman. Her hair this evening was a peculiar shade of pink. Last week it was blue. The week before that it was cyclamen-colored. She likes to experiment.

A quick phone call to the fire department disabused everyone of the idea that fire departments get cats out of trees anymore. They suggested putting an open can of cat food at the base of the tree and waiting for the kitten to come down on its own.

"Well, what would they do if it was someone's child up there?" Mrs. Ridgeway demanded. "Tell us to put out a bowl of cereal and hope the youngster came down by morning?!"

A large crowd gathered. Everyone had been out tending their gardens or sleeping on their porches, and they were glad for a little excitement. It always astonishes me how engrossed people are by marooned animals in hazardous circumstances.

Bobbie Boop and I trotted over to watch.

Two different people tried to climb the tree, but the trunk was too steep and there were no low limbs to grab onto. Old Mr. Wilkerson volunteered to get his slingshot and knock the kitten out of the tree. A chorus of disapproval sent him back to his front porch.

"Aw, hell," said one man, "don't worry about it. The cat'll get down on its own. How many dead cats you ever seen up in trees anyway?"

"Oh, but I couldn't bear to hear it cry like that all night," Mrs. Ridgeway told him.

Someone brought a big ladder. As they tried to lean it against the tree, I overheard a man and a woman talking on the sidewalk. "You know," said the woman, "I read an article recently that said if there's a nuclear war, only cats and cockroaches will survive."

"Well, then, who will be left to feed the cats?" asked the man.

"Oh, they'll live off the cockroaches," said the woman.

"I don't know about you," said the man, "but

my cat won't touch anything that doesn't come out of a can."

"Well, then," said the woman, with all seriousness, "I guess they'll have to resort to looting. There won't be anyone to keep them out of the supermarkets, will there?"

The ladder wasn't long enough, and the crowd was getting impatient. Meanwhile, the kitten had adapted to its situation and was staring down with eager curiosity at the crazed horde below.

"Where's Mrs. Pinchon when you need her?" someone shouted.

The Pinchons had gone boating for the day—Mrs. Pinchon would kick herself when she heard about *this*.

Looking up, I suddenly realized that the kitten was staring straight at us with a rapt expression: its eyes were full of fascination, as if it couldn't believe what it was seeing. Then I noticed that Bobbie Boop was staring up at *her* with a peculiar expression on *his* face. His soft, awestruck eyes looked as if they might melt right out of his head.

I could tell just by looking at the two of them—

It was love.

A brush with autumn this morning. You can tell big changes are on the way. Fewer mosquitoes the last couple of weeks; the grasshoppers are quieting down; the mornings are getting colder. It won't be long before Mrs. V is bringing out all the best blankets.

Only one fur ball today. Small one. More like a fur *glop*. When I lick myself, I can feel my winter coat starting to come in.

Mrs. Ridgeway was up most of the night trying to get the kitten down from the tree.

When I looked out the front window at midnight, she had a flashlight in one hand and was holding up and shaking what looked like a box of frozen fishsticks with the other.

At two-thirty she was waving what looked like a giant leg of lamb in the air.

I expected to see her with an entire cow or a live turkey in the yard an hour later, but she was sound asleep, wrapped in a blanket, at the base of the tree. Her head was resting against the trunk.

By sunrise both she and the kitten were gone.

The doorbell rang bright and early this morning.

Bobbie Boop and I peeked around Mrs. V's ankles to see who it was.

"I'm terribly sorry to bother you," said a petite and attractive woman in her thirties, "but I was wondering if you'd seen my grandmother . . ."

"Your grandmother?" Mrs. V asked.

"Yes, I'm Martha Miniver. Martha Mintucket Miniver. My grandmother is Mrs. Mintucket. She lives down the street from you . . ."

"Oh, yes, yes, of course. How do you do? No, I'm sorry, I haven't seen your grandmother in ages."

"Well, she's been missing for several days now, and we're very worried. I'm sure you know she doesn't go out much . . ."

"Oh, yes, yes, of course . . ."

". . . and we called the police but we thought it would be wise to check with everyone in the neighborhood . . ."

"Indeed . . ."

". . . just to make sure, you know, that she

didn't stop at someone's house for tea and decide to stay for a few days . . ."

"Of course . . ."

". . . and, well, you see, the last time I talked to her, she'd just bought these shoes, and, well, there's no denying she's been getting a bit dotty . . ."

"Aren't we all . . ."

". . . but she kept going on and on about buying these shoes, and I just couldn't understand why she . . ."

"No, of course not . . ."

". . . so we're all quite worried."

"Yes, I can see that."

There was a long pause.

"Well, you will call if you see her, won't you?" said Martha Miniver. "Here's my phone number."

"Oh, of course I will, the very instant I see her, if I see her, of course I will. . . ."

"She's wearing bright-red sneakers. High-tops. With some sort of . . . pump, I think."

"A pump," Mrs. V repeated with bewilderment. "I'll try to remember."

"Thanks so much."

Mrs. V closed the door.

"Martha Mintucket Miniver, Martha Mintucket Miniver," she kept repeating, until the words got all tangled up in her mouth. "Good Lord, what a tongue twister!"

The entire neighborhood must've heard the shouting in the Whittlesees' backyard this morning. Mr. Whittlesee was out yelling at his son.

"Get over here!" he thundered. "Did you hear me? Now!"

"What did I do, what did I do?" the boy cried.

There was screaming and sobbing, and Mrs. Whittlesee yelled, "The neighbors! Think of the neighbors!" from a back window.

"Haven't I told you a thousand times!" Mr. Whittlesee barked. "How many times have I told you?!"

"What did I do?" the boy begged.

"You think it's pretty funny, don't you?" Mr. Whittlesee snarled. "Huh? Huh? Well, you won't think it's very funny for long."

"Would you *please* think of the neighbors!" Mrs. Whittlesee shrieked.

"I didn't do anything, Daddy," the boy sobbed. "Don't hurt me. I'll be good. What did I do? I didn't do anything . . ."

"You ever listen to me?" Mr. Whittlesee yelled. "Are you deaf as well as stupid? Get inside. Right now. You understand me? Now!"

A door slammed shut and all was quiet again.

Was dozing in Mrs. Thornhill's backyard today, when I heard a small voice say, "Hello."

I looked up.

A single big eye blinked at me through the fence.

The Whittlesee boy was peeking at me from his backyard.

"Hello, kitty," he said.

He moved behind the fence and peered at me between the fence boards as he moved.

"Here, kitty-kitty," he called. "Come on, kitty," he said. "Don't you want to come say hello?"

I got up and stretched my front paws.

"That's it," he said. "Good kitty. I'd never hurt you, not in a million years. . . ."

He suddenly disappeared.

I tilted my head one way, then the other to see him. Then I leapt up on top of the fence.

He was standing on the grass with a book in his hand. He was wearing a pair of sunglasses that were too big for him. They gave his face a comical look.

"I won't hurt you, kitty," he said. "Come play with me."

He sat down on the grass and set his book aside.

I jumped off the fence. I sniffed a corner of the book.

"Good kitty," he said. He reached over and started lightly petting the top of my head. "You're a beautiful kitty. Such a beautiful, beautiful kitty."

I rubbed my chin against his knee and looked up at him. The sun was almost directly in my eyes.

"Don't run," he suddenly said. "Please, don't run away. Summer's over," he said sadly. "I wish summer lasted all year, don't you? I hate winter. It means I have to stay inside . . ."

I arched my back contentedly against his fingers.

He started petting me more vigorously. His hands were very sincere.

I crawled into his lap and curled up.

"I wish I were a kitty," he said. "If I were a kitty, then I could jump fences and go into other people's yards and climb trees. I could walk on everyone's roofs and explore the whole neighborhood that way. I could sail away on a little boat, just my own little raft, and everywhere I went people would be amazed at me."

He frisked my chin.

"Would you be my friend if I were a kitty?" he asked.

I looked up at his face again. This time I noticed a blotch on the right side of his cheek. Someone had clumsily smeared makeup on his face.

"You and I could sail all over the world together," he said. "And as soon as summer was done in one place, we'd sail away someplace else."

The wind came up, and a few leaves started to fall around us.

He curled his arms around me and kissed me on the top of the head.

"Don't run away," he said softly. "Everything'll be all right. Such a good, good kitty . . ."

Hard rain all day. Stayed inside. Mrs. V came into the living room and tried to read but fell asleep. Bobbie Boop crawled up onto her book and fell asleep, too, with his head nestled against her stomach. His tail looked like a long bookmark draped over the pages.

Within a few minutes, they were both snoring.

Sat on the rug. Watched them sleep. Felt happy.

More heavy rain. It was dark outside all day. The street in front of the house was like a river this afternoon with branches and garbage floating by. I watched a tin can sweep down the street with two grasshoppers bravely balanced on top of it.

By early evening, Bobbie Boop and I were almost out of our heads with boredom.

"All right, all right," Mrs. V announced "I can see the two of you are suffering."

She was holding her hands behind her back and had a funny smile on her face. She slowly brought her hands around in front and opened them.

Ping-Pong balls!

She tossed first one and then another into the far corners of the room, where they bounced against the wall, then the floor, then the wall, then the floor, then the wall, then the floor again.

She dropped a third one near my tail. It made several high bounces before hitting me on the rear end and rolling across the floor.

Bobbie Boop quickly captured one and was sitting protectively on top of it.

"No, no, no," Mrs. V told him, "that's no fun

at all." She got down on her hands and knees and pulled the ball out from under his belly. She tossed it across the room.

My ball rolled into her shoe. I stared at the ball, her, and the shoe unhappily.

"Well?" she said. "What do you want? Do you want me to throw it again? I'm not sure if I should. You haven't been a very good kitty lately."

She winked at me and then launched it across the floor.

I slid into Bobbie Boop while trying to catch it.

Mrs. V laughed.

The three of us played Ping-Pong balls for nearly an hour. Every time a ball got stuck, Mrs. V tossed it away again, sometimes into the next room, sometimes onto the sofa, sometimes up into the air with no idea where it would land.

Exhausted, she finally sat in the middle of the room and smiled.

But then the smile gradually disappeared and suddenly there were tears in her eyes. She slowly pulled herself up and went into the bedroom.

Bobbie Boop and I looked at each other.

We trotted after her.

She was sitting on the edge of the bed looking out the window at the rain.

We jumped up on the bed.

"Oh, God," she said, drawing us close, "you have no idea how much I adore the two of you, do you? You keep me feeling young!"

Bobbie Boop gently batted at a fold in her dress. I rubbed my head against her elbow.

Tonight she baked cookies, and the three of us curled up under a blanket and watched *The Ghost and Mrs. Muir.*

Clear today. Went outside. Ate too much grass. Threw it up—twice. Still felt hungry. Ate more grass. Shuffled inside feeling as if I weighed a hundred pounds.

Was out chasing leaves bright and early this morning. Bobbie Boop ran the length of the entire front yard with the same big leaf in his mouth—then he stopped so abruptly his rear end almost knocked his front paws out from under him.

He stared in rapture across the street.

Mrs. Ridgeway was out on her front porch with her new kitten.

"Now, now, Brigitte, stay close," said Mrs. Ridgeway. "We don't want any more little incidents . . ."

Brigitte, little bigger than a child's shoe, sat obediently on the porch. A swarm of tiny pink butterflies fluttered around her head. She blinked at the world with a mixture of innocence and obliviousness.

Bobbie Boop's chest heaved with a sigh.

"Pretty Brigitte," said Mrs. Ridgeway. "Such a noble kitty."

Brigitte tilted her head to the left. She tilted her head to the right. She turned her head slowly and licked her left shoulder. A tiny clump of hair stuck to her lips. She blinked. She looked as if there weren't a thought in her head.

"We aren't going to climb any more trees, now are we?" Mrs. Ridgeway told her. "Such a bad kitty to worry everyone like that!"

A bug landed on Brigitte's nose. Her eyes crossed.

Bobbie Boop was overcome. He flopped over on his side and twisted around on his back, first one way, then the other. Finally he lay on the sidewalk panting. His tail swept the ground excitedly.

"All right now, Brigitte," said Mrs. Ridgeway, "I'm going to pull a few weeds while you sit on the porch like a good kitty."

The bug having departed from her nose, Brigitte resumed blinking. She held her nose slightly aloft, as if she smelled someone cooking a hamburger somewhere.

"I'll be right down here where you can see me," Mrs. Ridgeway promised. She turned her back.

At that instant Brigitte bounded, without warning, off the porch. She bounced silently through the grass two or three times, and then sprinted effortlessly up the same big tree she'd been stuck in before.

"You just sit there and enjoy the sunshine," said Mrs. Ridgeway, who was intent on her crabgrass.

Brigitte hung by her claws from the trunk twenty feet above Mrs. Ridgeway's head. She had a deranged expression as if she didn't know what to do next, but then she pulled herself onto a high limb and sat there.

A flurry of dead bark fell into Mrs. Ridgeway's hair.

"Maybe someday, when you're bigger, you can climb trees again," said Mrs. Ridgeway, "but for now I think you'll enjoy life more if you just stay on the ground . . ."

Mrs. Ridgeway glanced up.

"Brigitte!" she cried.

Brigitte was climbing out to the end of a branch. The entire limb was swaying and bobbing precariously.

"Oh, Brigitte!" Mrs. Ridgeway gasped in dismay. "No, no. Bad Brigitte. Bad, bad, bad. Come down here at once. You *promised*."

Brigitte slipped. She looked for a moment like a monkey swinging from a tree.

"Brigitte," Mrs. Ridgeway moaned in frustration. She looked close to tears. "*Please,* come down. Don't put me through this."

A man sauntered by. He glanced over at Mrs. Ridgeway, then up into the tree, then at Mrs. Ridgeway again.

"Up there again, huh?" he said. "Lady, you ever figure that maybe that cat just doesn't *like* you?"

Mrs. Ridgeway turned white and looked as if she wanted to run sobbing into the house.

"I've had it!" she proclaimed in disgust. "That's the limit!" She grabbed her weed pail and her hand spade. "Stay up there!" she shouted. "You can rot up there for all I care!" She stomped into the house and slammed the door.

Fifteen minutes later she was outside again offering Brigitte catnip, caviar, fresh tuna, a Porterhouse steak, whatever it would take.

It was somewhere around the mention of a new kitty bed that Brigitte finally started to climb down.

Even when we're too young to understand everything that's being offered to us, cats excel at blackmail.

Sad day for the entire neighborhood. I looked out the window this afternoon, and there was Martha Mintucket Miniver walking slowly up the street. She was holding a muddy red sneaker in both hands. She was sobbing.

Mrs. Thornhill called through the kitchen window this morning while Mrs. V was doing the breakfast dishes.

"Did you hear about poor Mrs. Mintucket?" she shouted.

"Oh, yes," Mrs. V shouted back sadly. "The phone hasn't stopped ringing all morning!"

"I hear they haven't found her yet . . ."

"No, no sign of her yet."

". . . just the sneakers. In an irrigation ditch. About four blocks away . . ."

Mrs. V sighed. "I can't think for the world what might've happened to her."

"You don't suppose she was abducted, do you?" Mrs. T asked.

"Actually, I think she probably fell into the ditch and couldn't get out."

"Oh, it's just too horrible to contemplate," said Mrs. T. "And with all that rain recently. Who knows where . . ." Her voice trailed off.

Mrs. V was silent as she rinsed another plate.

"Did you know her well?" asked Mrs. T.

"No, not at all. She didn't socialize much."

"I hear she hadn't been out of her house in twenty years."

"Well, it's true that no one ever saw very much of her."

"Think of it," Mrs. T said. "She finally gets up the courage to leave her house, and something like *this* happens. What's *wrong* with the world these days?"

"Oh," Mrs. V said with a sigh, "I suppose it's the same world it always was. Everything always seems worse in the present than it did in the past . . ."

"Well, I for one am having extra locks put on my doors."

"Yes," Mrs. V replied, with a bit of regret in her voice, "I suppose many people will be doing that now . . ."

"Is that an automatic egg poacher you're washing?" Mrs. T suddenly asked, straining to see from her yard.

"Yes, it is."

"Oh, how do you like it? I've been thinking of getting one myself."

"Actually I don't care much for poached eggs," Mrs. V said, setting it aside to dry.

Mrs. T looked puzzled. "Then why do you have one?" she asked in bewilderment.

Bobbie Boop and I looked up from where we were enjoying our poached eggs on the floor.

"Oh," said Mrs. V, a bit flustered. "In case of company . . ."

"Oh, are you having company?" Mrs. T asked expectantly.

"No, no," Mrs. V replied. "I just thought I'd take it out and wash it. It's been getting dusty in the cabinets, you know."

"Oh," said Mrs. T. "Of course . . ."

They said good-bye, and Mrs. V turned away from the window and sat down at the breakfast table. She looked as if she was thinking rather sadly about the fate of Mrs. Mintucket.

First frost last night.

Went for a stroll in Mr. Butler's garden this afternoon.

An awful lot of his plants were lying in their beds looking like boiled spinach. The marigolds were gone, the impatiens were gone, the delphiniums were still standing but the blossoms had turned brown. There were only a few bugs out. Most of them were wandering around aimlessly. They looked disoriented.

Mr. Butler came out of the house while I was there and stood in the middle of his yard. "All that work," he mumbled to himself. "All those lovely summer days . . ."

He walked around the flower beds and inspected each group of plants. "It'll be six months before I see some of you again," he told them all sadly.

Suddenly he leaned over and peered deep into the climbing roses, where I was hiding. Our eyes met. He gave me a long, affectionate smile.

"You've had a good time in the garden this summer, haven't you?" he said. "All the cats in the neighborhood have. A gardener can always tell how successful he's been by the number of cats who come to visit . . ."

His friend, Mr. Fielding, called for him from inside and, with a final wistful glance at the yard, Mr. Butler went back into the house.

Tonight the entire neighborhood was full of the smell of baking. Brownies, cookies, cakes— everyone must've taken out their baking pans all at once.

Bobbie Boop refused to come in last night. Mrs. V was very worried. "Foolish cat," she muttered after trying all evening to get him in. All through dinner I could see her glancing anxiously out the window.

She went out after him at least half a dozen times after that. Each time she came back, she looked more unhappy. "I know he's just sitting out there in the bushes watching me," she said. "What in the world's gotten into him?"

She finally went to bed. But she got up again around two. She went outside with a flashlight.

"Bobbie Boop," she called in a loud whisper. She searched through the bushes. "Bobbie Boop, come inside! Bobbie Boop, where are you? Oh, Bobbie Boop, *please* come in . . ."

There was no sign of him.

"How am I supposed to sleep not knowing where he is?" she said, crawling back into bed and turning out the light.

"Cats!" I heard her lament in the darkness.

I went into the living room and jumped into a front window. Sat there for a long time.

Bobbie Boop was fine—I could see him.

He was sitting across the street on Mrs. Ridgeway's porch waiting for a glimpse of Brigitte.

Two policemen came to the house today to ask questions about Mrs. Mintucket.

"Would you like some tea, coffee, soda pop?" Mrs. V said as she showed them into the living room.

"No, ma'am," said the one.

The other stopped and looked straight at me with an unpleasant expression. "This cat vaccinated for rabies, ma'am?" he asked.

"Why, yes, of course," said Mrs. V, blinking at him uncertainly. "Why do you ask?"

"Just wanted to make sure," he said. "It's the law in this county."

"Oh, of course . . ."

"Cats carry more rabies than any other animal on the planet, ma'am," he explained.

"You don't say."

"They also carry at least a dozen other potentially lethal diseases including cat scratch fever, staphylococcus, and toxoplasmosis. Toxoplasmosis will make you insane, ma'am."

Mrs. V laughed a little nervously. "Perhaps that accounts for why so many of my friends think I'm crazy," she said.

Neither one of the policemen smiled.

"Some people believe cats should be outlawed as household pets," he told her grimly.

"I'm sure they must all be very charming people," Mrs. V said, trying to make conversation.

"Cats were responsible for the Black Plague, you know, ma'am."

"I thought it was rats," she said.

"That's what *some* people would like you to think," he told her in a sinister tone full of implications.

"Well, I'm sure you didn't come all this way just to discuss my cats," said Mrs. V.

"*Cats?*" he repeated. "You have more than one?"

Mrs. V looked rattled. "Yes. I do. I have two actually."

"You aren't planning on having kittens, are you, ma'am?" he asked.

"Oh, no," she said, laughing gaily. "My kitten-bearing days are behind me."

"You have to have a license to breed cats in this county," he told her. "It's a serious offense if you don't."

"I'll keep that in mind," she replied. "But mine are both fixed. I mean, one of them's fixed. The other *will* be soon. He's still too young."

"Make sure you have him checked for worms and other dangerous parasites when you do, ma'am."

"I will," she said, looking suddenly fatigued.

They stayed for another fifteen minutes.

Halfway through their questions about Mrs. Mintucket, Bobbie Boop came into the living room. He was dragging one of Mrs. V's panty hose behind him. He had the waistband firmly between his teeth and was making trilling noises as he straddled the fabric and tiptoed across the floor.

The policemen stared at him in alarm, then looked at Mrs. V disapprovingly.

"He's getting his costume ready for Halloween," Mrs. V told them with a smile.

Spent the morning on top of the TV. I sometimes wonder if people who make TVs design them with cats in mind—not too high, not too low, always warm. A perfect place to perch.

Watched a speck on the wall for almost an hour. Slept.

"No one is going out now," Mrs. V told us in the afternoon. "I don't want to worry about getting the two of you in before nightfall."

Lots of trick-or-treaters tonight. Strange how people delight in pretending to be something they're not. Can't imagine cats ever enjoying that—putting on fake whiskers or artificial ears to look like someone or something else.

One boy came to the door dressed as a cat. I noticed Mrs. V gave him more candy than other children.

She had no sooner closed the door than the doorbell rang again.

"They're coming in droves," she said cheerfully as she reached for her bags of candy.

She opened the door.

No one was there. There was a brown shopping bag on the doorstep.

"Good grief, someone left their treat bag on the porch," she said peering out into the darkness.

The bag suddenly moved.

Mrs. V turned white.

"Good Lord," she gasped.

It moved again.

"Dear God . . ."

The bag fell over on its side and began moving so insistently it looked as if it might start walking across the porch.

"What kind of prank is this?" she asked.

She looked out into the yard to find the perpetrator. No one was there.

Finally she knelt down. She regarded the bag with caution. Then she opened it. She held it at arm's length while peeking into it.

"Oh, how horrible!" she gasped.

She quickly brought the bag into the house and closed the door.

She rushed the bag into the bedroom and sat down next to it on the bed. Then she gently pulled out the contents.

There was a black-and-white cat, so thin and

frail its spine was visible and its legs were like twigs. Its face was filthy.

It looked at Mrs. V and meowed at her pathetically.

"We can't just turn this cat back out onto the streets and hope for the best," Mrs. V told us this morning. "Sometimes hope needs a little nudge."

She tried to feed it several times today. But it just sat in the window and stared out at the street.

Bobbie Boop went up and sniffed the tip of its tail. He got a very peculiar look on his face and backed away with his mouth hanging open.

"You have to eat *something*," Mrs. V finally told the cat. She took him into the kitchen and gave him some yogurt mixed with anchovies. He ate a little, but then returned to the window.

Tonight Mrs. V tried to take him to bed with her. He sat on the bed watching her put on her nightgown and fluff her pillows. He watched her put an extra blanket on the bed, and he sat while she read for a few minutes. But as soon as the light was out, he was gone.

He sat in the front window all night staring out at the street with an unhappy look on his face.

"Zachary!" Mrs. V announced this afternoon. "That's what we'll call him—Zachary."

She looked as if she was about to pick him up and waltz around the room with him, but something in his look stopped her. Instead, she smiled and petted him gently as he sat in the window. "Zachary, Zachary, Zachary," she told him. "Do you like that name?"

Zachary was lying on some towels in the laundry room this evening. He looked half dead.

Tonight I heard Mrs. V saying his name as she was getting ready for bed. I thought he must be in the room with her. But he was sitting in the living-room window.

I went into the bedroom.

Mrs. V was sitting on the edge of the bed with a photograph in her hands.

"Oh, Zachary," I heard her murmur. "My beautiful, beautiful Zachary. Oh, Zachary . . ."

Got up early this morning. Helped Mrs. V make coffee.

"Just what every cup of coffee needs," Mrs. V said, deftly removing a cat hair from the handle of her cup.

Sat and read the paper with her. Crawled between the pages and stuck my head out looking for affection. "It must be an exhausting life," she said, "devoting oneself to the pursuit of perfect cuteness." She reached under the paper and scratched my back.

I helped her make the bed after that. Chased the corners of the sheets all around the mattress.

"You're certainly being attentive today," Mrs. V remarked.

I rolled on my back hoping for a belly rub.

"Ah," she said. "So we need a little reassurance, do we?" She gently scratched my stomach. "We aren't quite as freewheeling as we'd like to think . . ."

In the afternoon she sat on the sofa and read.

I curled up next to her.

After an hour, she frisked my chin and stroked my back. "Such good behavior today," she commented. "You haven't clawed a single one of the pages."

This evening we watched *The Lion in Winter*. It wasn't what I expected, but the music was nice. I sat in Mrs. V's lap until she got up to go to bed.

"It's all right," she said, patting me on the head. "I've had a day or two myself when my only ambition was to inspire a little love . . ."

She kissed me on the head and went into the bedroom.

"Listen, my little one," Mrs. V told Zachary this morning when he took up his regular watch in the living-room window. "Whoever it is you're waiting for isn't coming back."

He looked up at her and meowed.

"I'm sorry," she said. "If I knew who they were, I'd try and find them for you."

He rubbed his head against her hand. He was purring.

"Zachary, listen to me," she said taking his head in her hands and kneeling down so their eyes were level. "This is your home now. Those other people are never coming back for you. They left you here . . . for a reason. Now, please, Zachary—come away from the window."

She picked him up and took him into the den, where she was sorting papers. He curled up on the carpet next to her and fell asleep. She kept glancing over at him to make sure he was still there.

He's one of the strangest cats I've ever seen. He doesn't play; he doesn't eat. He acts most of the time as if Bobbie Boop and I aren't even here.

Bobbie Boop was busy digging in the front garden this morning.

Later I saw him trot across the street with some sort of bug in his mouth. He sat down on the Ridgeways' porch, right in front of the front door. He waited.

Mrs. Ridgeway finally came out around noon. She looked at him in surprise.

"What are you doing here?" she asked. "Who are you? Shoo. Shoo!"

He didn't move.

"Did you hear me?" she demanded. "Shoo!"

He still didn't move.

"Did you hear me, buster?" she told him. "Take a hike. Skedaddle! On your way! Git! Hit the road!"

He finally turned around and went slowly down the porch steps.

He looked crestfallen.

Mrs. Thornhill has gotten a dog.

"I suppose she's nervous after this dreadful business with Mrs. Mintucket," Mrs. V said this morning. "You know, though, it doesn't exactly look like a dog. I'm not sure *what* it looks like. But I *don't* think it's a dog."

". . . No, no, he's full-grown," Mrs. Thornhill was telling someone on the phone this morning while she was raking leaves in her front yard. "I didn't want to go through the ordeal of raising a puppy. They chew on *everything.* No, I got him through a want ad in the newspaper. His name is Vlad," she said. "I'm not sure why they named him that. . . ."

Vlad is about twice the size of the Morgans' black Labrador, Ralph, and when he yawns you can see he has teeth like a chain saw.

This afternoon Vlad was eating a giant hole in Mrs. Thornhill's back fence.

First snow.

Bobbie Boop went charging from window to window trying to catch snowflakes through the glass.

"It *is* lovely, isn't it?" said Mrs. V. "By February I'll hate it. But for now it's simply beautiful."

Snow always looks like fun until you get out in it. The flakes disappear as soon as you catch them, and then you're left sitting there with a cold, wet nose.

The four of us watched *Doctor Zhivago* tonight.

Bobbie Boop and Zachary slept underneath Mrs. V's blanket through most of it.

"Oh, do come out from there," Mrs. V finally said. "I worry you'll asphyxiate . . ."

She pulled them out, and the three of us watched the rest of the movie curled up together on her lap.

Thanksgiving Day. Mrs. V had neighbors over for dinner. Mr. Butler and Mr. Fielding came, dressed in almost identical suits.

"Ah, one of my favorite cats," Mr. Butler said when he spotted me on the dining-room buffet. He scratched one of my ears.

"You enjoy cats so much," said Mrs. V as she hung up his coat, "I'm surprised you don't have one of your own."

"Alas," he replied sadly. "It's a long story."

Mr. Fielding handed her a bouquet of flowers and a bottle of wine.

Mrs. V held the flowers in front of my nose. "These are to look at, *not* to eat," she warned. She put them in a vase on the dining-room table.

Mrs. Thornhill and her daughter came also. Mrs. Thornhill was wearing an old lambskin coat.

"Oh," she said as everyone admired it, "I just thought I'd take it out of the closet for old times' sake . . ." She modeled it exuberantly. She held a sleeve up to my nose. "Mmm, lambskin," she said. "If I'm not careful, you'll have *me* for dinner."

Her daughter was dressed in torn jeans and a T-shirt.

"I tried to get her to wear something nice," I overheard Mrs. T complain when she was alone with Mrs. V in the kitchen. "But you know how it's been . . ."

"Oh, it's Thanksgiving!" said Mrs. V. "The only important thing is that we're all here and everyone's well."

Mrs. T gave her a little hug.

"Are the Ridgeways coming?" Mr. Butler asked.

Bobbie Boop's ears perked up.

"No, no," said Mrs. V, filling everyone's wineglass. "They're out of town for the holiday. . . ."

Bobbie Boop's ears slumped.

"Who is this?" Mr. Fielding asked as he petted Zachary.

"Oh, it's a terrible, terrible story," Mrs. V told him. "He was left on my doorstep Halloween night. In a paper bag."

"A paper bag?!" Mrs. Thornhill asked.

"He's just now gaining some weight," said Mrs. V. "He's such a sad little cat. But he's a sweetheart."

She kissed Zachary on the head.

"Three cats," said Mr. Butler. "If you aren't careful, you'll wind up like the Pinchons."

"Oh, I think all my life I've wanted to be an eccentric," said Mrs. V. "If you only could have heard the two policemen who came the other day to ask about . . ." She hesitated. ". . . Mrs. Mintucket."

Everyone looked down at their drinks.

"On and on they went about how dangerous cats are, and I'll catch this disease and that disease and will wind up with worms!"

"Has there been any news about Mrs. Mintucket?" Mrs. Thornhill asked.

"I'm not even sure they're still looking," said Mr. Butler.

"Poor Mrs. Mintucket . . ." said Mrs. T.

Mrs. V served dinner a short time later. When she brought out the turkey, everyone applauded. She set it down in the middle of the dining-room table.

Bobbie Boop immediately jumped up next to it.

"No, dear," Mrs. V said. She picked him up and put him on the floor.

He jumped back on the table again.

"No," she told him firmly. "Be a good boy, and you'll get some leftovers."

"Perhaps you should have set places for them," Mr. Butler suggested.

"Oh, don't think such things don't cross my mind now and then," said Mrs. V.

Throughout dinner Bobbie Boop and I wandered beneath the chairs. It was like a cloudburst of food. Everyone gave us so many scraps we didn't know which chair to go to next.

Zachary sat alone in the living room, but then he came into the dining room and jumped on Mr. Butler's lap.

Everyone stopped and looked at him.

He curled up and set his head down to sleep.

"You don't need to keep him there," Mrs. V said politely. "You can put him down if you want . . ."

"I don't have the heart to," said Mr. Butler, who went on eating.

Toward the end of dinner, Mr. Fielding suddenly looked at his watch and said, "Do you mind if I turn on the weather for a moment?"

"No, no, not at all," said Mrs. V.

He got up and went into the living room and turned on the television.

"Mr. Fielding has to go north tomorrow," said Mr. Butler, "and he's concerned about snow."

"Business or pleasure?" asked Mrs. V.

"A little of both, if I know Mr. Fielding," said Mr. Butler.

Suddenly there was a gasp from the living room.

"Come in here!" Mr. Fielding shouted. "Come in here at once. Everyone! Come look at this . . ."

Everyone got up from the table and ran to the television.

There on the TV was Mrs. Mintucket. She was walking briskly along a desolate highway that seemed to extend forever into the distance. The road was surrounded by sagebrush and desert.

"Oh, my God," gasped Mrs. Thornhill.

"Good Lord," said Mrs. V.

A reporter was struggling to keep up with Mrs. Mintucket as she marched down the road.

"Mrs. Mintucket, Mrs. Mintucket," he panted, "why have you chosen this time to walk barefoot across America?"

He thrust the microphone into her face. "To prove to the world that the shoes do not make the man! Or the woman!" she said.

"Where in the world is she?" asked Mrs. Thornhill excitedly.

"It looks like Nevada or Arizona," said Mr. Butler in awe.

"What made you decide to do this now, Mrs. Mintucket?" asked the reporter. "Is it the state of the world? Do you think there's too much emphasis put on fashion in American culture?"

"Twenty years I sat waiting for the right pair of shoes to set me free," she proclaimed. "And all the time it wasn't shoes I needed, but courage! Freedom lies in your feet, not what you put on them!"

"What does your family think of your crusade, Mrs. Mintucket?" asked the reporter.

"Young man," she told him, "the moment I realized what I must do I left my old life behind. I haven't stopped walking, and I've never looked back. One must do that in a crusade, you know!''

The reporter stopped, and Mrs. Mintucket marched off into the distance.

"And that's it from Dalhart, Texas," said the TV reporter, "where Mrs. Miriam Mintucket, a seventy-two-year-old grandmother, continues her barefoot march across America, taking her crusade all the way to the Pacific Coast! Back to you, Fred and Norma . . .''

"Miriam Mintucket, Miriam Mintucket," Mrs. V muttered. "They're certainly fond of alliteration in that family!"

"She's a celebrity!" gasped Mrs. Thornhill.

"Good grief," said Mr. Butler. "Someone call her granddaughter."

"Oh, I'm certain her phone's ringing off the hook as we speak," said Mrs. V.

Everyone returned to the dining room chattering about Mrs. Mintucket.

As Mrs. V sat down, her eyes suddenly grew wide and she blinked several times as if she couldn't believe what she was seeing.

A tail was sticking out from the turkey.

"Bobbie Boop!" she exclaimed in dismay.

Bobbie Boop had crawled inside the turkey and was happily eating his fill.

At the sound of Mrs. V's voice he tried to back out all at once and nearly took the turkey over the edge of the dining-room table.

"Oh, my God," said Mrs. V, trying to pull him out. "I'm so sorry," she apologized to everyone. "Oh, really, I'm terribly, terribly sorry."

"Oh, I'd had quite enough anyway," Mr. Butler said philosophically.

"I'm stuffed," said Mrs. Thornhill.

Mrs. Thornhill's daughter was laughing so hard there were tears coming down her face.

Mrs. V pulled and pulled, and finally dislodged Bobbie Boop from the turkey. When his head popped out, his mouth was full to overflowing with meat.

"Let's move on to the pie," Mr. Butler suggested.

"Oh, yes, the pie," said Mrs. V, looking relieved.

"Pie! I love pie!" said Mr. Fielding.

Mrs. V took the turkey and Bobbie Boop into the kitchen.

Zachary and I followed and sat on the kitchen floor.

Mrs. V shook her head and looked at us.

"I wish I were thirty again," she said, "so I'd have fifty more Thanksgivings to tell *this* story."

Then she patted us all on the head and carried the pies out to the table.

WINTER

Mrs. Thornhill's daughter came over this morning.

"My mother wants to borrow your card table," she said.

"Oh, certainly," said Mrs. V.

"She's playing bridge this afternoon," Mrs. Thornhill's daughter explained.

"I enjoy a hand of bridge myself now and then," said Mrs. V.

"Our dog ate the only card table we had."

"I'm so sorry," said Mrs. V, pulling a card table from the hall closet. "But, you know, sometimes a little duct tape is all it takes to repair things."

Mrs. Thornhill's daughter blinked at her. "You don't understand," she told Mrs. V. "He *ate* it. The whole thing. It was there one minute, gone the next."

Mrs. V turned a little pale.

"A week ago he ate our lawn furniture," said Mrs. Thornhill's daughter. "And yesterday my mother caught him with the vacuum cleaner in his mouth!"

"Perhaps you should consider a muzzle," said Mrs. V.

"We did," Mrs. Thornhill's daughter told her. "He ate it."

"Are you quite sure you're safe over there with that animal?" Mrs. V asked.

"Oh, he likes *us,*" Mrs. T's daughter told her. "It's other people we have to worry about. Thanks for the card table. . . ."

This afternoon I was looking out the front window and suddenly saw Mrs. Thornhill's friends run screaming out her front door.

"That's *no* dog," Mrs. V commented grimly over my shoulder.

Tonight, the "dog" spent hours baying at the full moon.

More snow today. It fell for hours. By late morning, the lawn was buried. By noon, the flower beds were gone. By early afternoon, the junipers were only a memory—they looked like a herd of white turtles sitting in the front yard.

Went looking for a little excitement around the house.

Tried climbing the bedroom drapes, but it wasn't any fun. I felt I was just going through the motions.

Tried clawing the ironing board—Mrs. V forgot to put it away. It quickly fell over, fabric side down. That was the end of that.

Finally joined Mrs. V on the sofa. She had dozed off while reading. "Oh, it's you," she said with a start when I jumped on her chest. "I don't know what's wrong with me today. I don't feel quite myself. . . ."

She stroked my back, then drifted off again.

Bobbie Boop was asleep on top of the refrigerator. Zachary was sleeping on one of the heating ducts.

I jumped up on the dining-room table. Suddenly felt agitated.

Started to meow. The meows became cater-wauls.

"What on earth is the matter?!" said Mrs. V, racing into the room. "What's happened? What's wrong?!"

I looked up at her in distress.

I'd just had my first taste of cabin fever.

Mrs. V got our Christmas tree today. Nice big one with long branches. It reaches all the way to the ceiling.

"Well, we need a big tree to accommodate all the extra presents this year," she said. "After all, there are three of you now."

Two deliverymen brought it inside.

Bobbie Boop sat on the floor near the base of it and looked up agog. I envied him his first Christmas.

Tonight the four of us decorated it. Zachary and Bobbie Boop helped put on the garlands—then helped take them off again. I helped reposition several ornaments after Mrs. V had hung them on the branches. Bobbie Boop ran off with the Christmas angel, and Mrs. V had to chase him under the bed to get it back.

"Believe it or not," she said, "I *would* like to curb some of this nonsense . . ."

Later we baked Christmas cookies.

Mrs. V made some of them to hang on the tree. She took each of our paws and pressed them into the dough. Then she wrote our names underneath in red speckles.

Is there any time of the year a cat loves more?

Was sleeping in the front window this morning. Suddenly woke up and saw a pair of tiny cat eyes blinking back at me through the glass.

Jumped up. Hissed. Howled.

The cat on the other side of the glass looked at me in confusion.

It was Brigitte.

As soon as Bobbie Boop saw her, he jumped up. He nearly knocked me out of the window.

Brigitte gazed at him tenderly.

Bobbie Boop made little mewing sounds.

Suddenly Mrs. Ridgeway appeared.

"Are you *trying* to turn me into a madwoman!" she demanded. "Is that what you want?"

Brigitte looked up at her imploringly.

"I leave the door open for ten seconds, and you disappear! Bad, bad, bad!" Mrs. Ridgeway cried, snatching her from the window. "You'll only be happy when I'm sick from worry, won't you?!"

She marched back across the street.

"I'm never letting you out of my sight again!" Mrs. Ridgeway scolded her.

Was outside today. Everywhere I went there was the sound of melting snow. Mr. Wilkerson was out knocking icicles off his gutters with his slingshot.

Mrs. Thornhill and her daughter drove up as I was sitting on the sidewalk.

"Why don't you just stay here with me?" Mrs. T was saying as she got out of the car. "The two of you could live here . . ."

"Mother . . ."

"You wouldn't have to pay rent—at least not until he got a good job. . . ."

"Mother . . ."

"You think it's going to be easy, the two of you living on your own? No income. No furniture. You're both teenagers, for God's sake. Teenagers!"

"Mother, stop it!"

"I just hate the thought that this is our last Christmas together," said Mrs. T.

"Mother, you're making me angry."

"I don't want to be alone!" Mrs. T suddenly bellowed. She stood in the snow, her arms full of packages. "I don't *deserve* to be alone!"

There was a long silence.

"I'll ask him what he thinks of the idea," her daughter finally muttered.

Mrs. T turned and started into the house. "It doesn't matter," she snapped. "I can't stand the sight of him anyway. Forget I ever mentioned it."

"Grow up, Mother," the daughter moaned. "Just grow up . . ."

"You mean grow old and quit making a fuss about it, don't you?" Mrs. T complained before she closed the front door.

Tried to help Mrs. V wrap Christmas presents this afternoon. I chased the edges of the wrapping paper as she unrolled it. Mrs. V pushed me away. "I really don't need your assistance right now, thank you very much," she said.

Zachary jumped up on the table to watch. He seemed interested in the tape dispenser. He batted it twice, then got his paw stuck in some tape, and when he tried to pull away he unwound several feet of it and yanked the entire roll out of the dispenser.

"Oh, that's just wonderful," said Mrs. V. "Here, give me your paw. Good grief!"

Bobbie Boop jumped up on the table, too. He yawned so wide his mouth looked bigger than his whole head for a moment. He'd just had a nice nap. The red ribbon instantly caught his eye. He stared at it for a few seconds before finally pouncing. He knocked the roll on the floor, and a long piece of it unwound as it sailed away across the carpet.

"All right, that's enough!" said Mrs. V. "All of you—off the table. Right now! Go! Go!"

The telephone rang.

She sighed.

"Off the table!" she commanded as she walked away.

When she came back, Zachary was completely bound up in tape, Bobbie Boop had unraveled all the ribbon and was trotting down the hall with one end of it in his mouth, and I was eating the wrapping paper.

"Oh, my God!" said Mrs. V. "What are you doing?!"

She finally herded all three of us into the bedroom.

"Pandemonium, thy name is cat," she declared as she closed the door.

Mrs. V very sick. She fell on the front steps this morning and had to be taken away in an ambulance.

We're alone here now.

Bobbie Boop and Zachary stay close to me.

Why doesn't anyone think to tell us what's going on?

Mrs. Thornhill came in this morning to pack a small suitcase of Mrs. V's belongings.

Bobbie Boop jumped into the middle of the suitcase as she was trying to put clothes in it.

She picked him up and put him on the floor.

He jumped into the middle of the suitcase again.

"Listen, you," she said, "I don't have time for this." She tossed him on the bed and rummaged through Mrs. V's closet.

When she turned around, Bobbie Boop was in the suitcase again.

She stood for a moment studying him. Finally, she picked him up and sat down on the edge of the bed.

"Your mother will be home soon," she told him. "She's had a minor stroke. She's going to be fine, though. She just has to be careful . . ."

She caressed his head and held him for a moment, then finished packing and left.

It turned bitter cold this evening. The three of us spent the night huddled together on the sofa.

Long nap this afternoon. Was awakened by the sound of Zachary roaming from room to room. He was meowing unhappily.

He pawed at the door to Mrs. V's study for a long time.

Then he went into the bedroom and wandered across the top of her dressing table. He rubbed himself against all her bottles and brushes.

He came into the living room and sat for a long time staring at me.

Then he went away.

When I last saw him, he was sound asleep on Mrs. V's pillow.

What is to become of us?

"There's been a little problem," Mrs. Thornhill told us this morning.

It seems Mrs. V won't be coming home right away.

"But an old friend is coming to take care of you," Mrs. T announced.

Aunt Petra? I thought to myself.

"Mrs. Axe," said Mrs. T. "Lillian Axe. She and Mrs. Vigil have known each other for years. She's flying in from Montana this evening."

Mrs. Axe arrived just before nightfall. She's a huge, towering woman in her midseventies. She has the biggest hands and feet I've ever seen. She smells of mothballs and chlorine bleach.

She put her luggage down in the living room and glanced around in dismay.

"Well, here we are," said Mrs. T brightly. She looked quite puny standing next to Mrs. Axe.

"Where exactly do you live in Montana?" Mrs. T asked, fussing with the house keys. Mrs. Axe seemed to make her nervous.

"Bluehare," said Mrs. Axe in a voice like a growl.

"I beg your pardon . . ."

"Hare as in rabbit," Mrs. Axe growled. "Bluehare."

"Oh, I thought you meant . . ."

Mrs. Axe, standing there with a full head of blue hair, didn't smile.

She suddenly spied the three of us sitting together on the sofa.

"I don't have much use for cats," she said grimly.

"Oh, they're very nice cats," Mrs. T told her. "I think they're probably the nicest cats I've ever known."

"This one looks diseased," said Mrs. Axe, pointing an accusing finger at Zachary.

"Oh, he's just a little sweetheart," said Mrs. T. "Why, just a month ago he was all skin and bones, and Mrs. V has worked her heart out to . . ."

Mrs. T's voice faded off.

Mrs. Axe was glaring at her.

"I've never related much to animals," Mrs. Axe announced with finality. "I don't have the kind of insecurities that necessitate cozying up to—" She got a sour look on her face "—furry things."

"Well, they're Mrs. Vigil's darlings," Mrs. T replied. "She just adores them."

"She shouldn't have cats at her age," Mrs. Axe told her. "She could trip over them. I'll talk to her about getting rid of them."

Mrs. T said nothing. She had a look of horror on her face.

"We should go to the hospital now," said Mrs. Axe.

She returned alone a few hours later. She made herself a sandwich and sat down in front of the television. She watched a documentary on capital punishment.

Mrs. Axe discovered Bobbie Boop playing with a rubber band in the bathtub this evening. "Cats are *not* allowed in the bathroom," she announced. She closed the door. The bathroom is off-limits now. Bobbie Boop will miss his afternoon naps in the sink. Zachary will miss watching the toilet flush.

Mrs. Axe went to bed early.

Sometime in the middle of the night she started moaning, as if she had bad indigestion. A minute later there was a series of piercing screams.

She flung open the bedroom door. She stood in the doorway, in her nightgown, looking pale and shaken. She was panting for air, and her disheveled hair and worried eyes made her look a thousand years old. She gripped the door frame as if she couldn't stand up on her own.

Bobbie Boop suddenly scampered out from between her feet.

"Stay out!" she roared. "If I ever find you under my covers again, I'll . . . I'll . . ."

She quivered all over with rage.

She slammed the door.

Was locked in the broom closet all afternoon. I was climbing around behind the vacuum cleaner when the door suddenly slammed shut.

I meowed.

There was no response.

I scratched at the door.

Still no response.

I banged the broom several times against the door.

Nothing.

Dozed off in frustration.

Woke with a start a short time later. Started banging on the door in earnest. Yowled. Knocked everything I could off the shelf above me. Stuck a paw under the door to attract attention. Flung a vacuum cleaner attachment against the door as hard as I could.

The door opened.

Mrs. Axe regarded me with annoyance. "*What* are you doing in there?" she bellowed.

I bolted out.

"Isn't there enough to keep you occupied in the rest of the house," she asked, "without your climbing into the closets and making a mess of everything?"

I gave her one of my best dirty looks and walked away.

"Closets are off-limits to cats!" she growled.

Mrs. Thornhill was out yelling at her "dog" in the backyard this morning.

"Oh, no! Not the locust tree! Not the *entire* locust tree!" she shrieked.

I thought her yard looked as though it had fewer trees in it these days.

Mrs. Ridgeway came over to introduce herself to Mrs. Axe this afternoon.

"It's so good of you to come all the way from Wyoming to help Mrs. Vigil in her hour of need," said Mrs. Ridgeway.

"Montana," Mrs. Axe corrected her. "I'm from Montana, not Wyoming."

"It's always so much harder when these things happen this time of year, isn't it?" said Mrs. Ridgeway.

"They're two different states," said Mrs. Axe.

Mrs. Ridgeway blinked at her. "What?" she asked.

"Montana and Wyoming. They're two different states."

"Why, yes," said Mrs. Ridgeway, looking baffled. "Of course, they are . . ."

"I'm from Montana. It isn't the same thing as Wyoming at all."

"Well, I didn't say it was," said Mrs. Ridgeway, flushing slightly.

"Montana's Big Sky Country," said Mrs. Axe. "Wyoming has hardly any sky at all."

"Well, yes, now that you point it out to me . . ." said Mrs. Ridgeway. "And how do you like *our* little corner of the world?"

Mrs. Axe looked as grim as a snake with bad indigestion.

Strange dreams last night. I dreamt of my mother. Her face was soft and beautiful and kind. She smelled of roses and catnip. I wanted her to lick my ears, but she turned away and ran out the door. I tried to run after her, but she always stayed a few feet ahead of me. Finally she disappeared into thin air.

Mrs. Axe took her usual bath this morning. She goes into the bathroom with a bottle of chlorine bleach. When she comes out, the bottle is empty. I think she bathes in it.

Sunday night tonight and no television. Mrs. Axe read a book. We sat on the floor and watched her.

"Quit looking at me like that," she finally snapped.

She reads a book in the most peculiar way. She turns each page as if she was thinking of ripping it out.

Mrs. V has been gone a week, but there's no news about her condition. Mrs. Axe goes to the hospital twice a day but tells us nothing.

Mrs. Axe let me out this morning.

I sensed she was hoping I wouldn't come back.

She wouldn't let Bobbie Boop out. "You're not big enough," she said, shutting the door in his face.

Prowled around the neighborhood. Not many people on the streets. No conversations to listen to, no one to watch. It seems like all the neighborhood's secrets have moved indoors for the winter.

Mrs. Pinchon was taking garbage out of her house. Her eyes lit up when she saw me coming down the sidewalk—but then she looked disappointed. "Oh, it's you," she said in an irritated voice and turned away.

She'd left a side door to her house open. I've always wondered what her house was like, so I dashed inside while her back was turned.

Found myself in a huge, dark kitchen. It smelled of milk and tuna fish.

Passed by an endless row of little white food dishes with names on them: Serafina, Amanda, Spitfire, Snowball, Munchkin, Mindy. . . . Stopped to take a sip from a water bowl the size of a small bathtub. Someone had dropped his rubber mouse in it.

A large orange cat was sitting on top of the refrigerator, batting grapes onto the floor while another cat sat below smashing each one as it landed.

They ignored me.

Went down a long hallway.

The living room was full of cats—cats on the tables, cats on the china cabinets, cats in the bookcases. Three cats, all black, were curled up together on the sofa; it was an odd sight, like a single black creature with three heads. Two kittens were on a side table tearing apart a lamp shade—they took turns spinning the shade and then yanking off the fabric.

No one paid any attention to me. I guess they've become numb to the sight of a new face.

Mrs. Pinchon suddenly cried, "Be-ooootiful cat, wonderful cat!" from the kitchen.

I ducked behind a chair.

She was carrying a huge Siamese into the living room. The cat rolled playfully in her arms and reached for her nose with its paws. "Be-ooootiful, be-ooootiful cat," Mrs. Pinchon chanted. "Charming cat, exquisite cat, lovely cat, mysterious cat. Oh, you're just too wonderful for words. How can you stand being so mysterious and be-ooootiful? Cat, cat, cat, cat . . ."

She put it on the sofa and went back into the kitchen.

Everyone looked quite happy. Very pampered and contented. Given their expressions from the front windows sometimes, I'd expected them to look like detainees at a refugee camp.

Went upstairs.

Mr. Pinchon started up the stairs right behind me.

"One of these days," he muttered as he passed me, "I'm going to trip and fall over one of you, and *then* who's going to give you your little treats at night?"

A cat was sleeping inside a big ceramic pot at the top of the stairs. All you could see were the tips of its ears. The ears rotated to follow my sound as I passed by.

In the master bedroom there was a cat, obviously old and frail, who had been set up in its own beautiful basket with an ornate silk blanket. With its delicate face and ancient eyes, it looked like some regal, aging empress installed on a bed of unbelievable luxury.

It had a look of uncomplaining patience.

It mewed at me gently.

"Puff!" Mr. Pinchon called from the door. "Oh, Puff," he said sadly. He came in to pet her.

He didn't even glance at me.

"How are you, Puff?" he asked. He knelt down and rubbed his head against hers.

Her eyes softened in deep contentment. She stretched her chin as he ran his finger up her neck.

"Feeling any better?" he asked. "Oh, Puff, I wish there were something I could do for you." He held his cheek tenderly against her. "Puff, Puff, Puff." He sighed. He scratched her back. "My wonderful, wonderful Puff. I'll always love you . . ."

She gazed at him with what was obviously the adoration of a lifetime.

His hand trembled a little as he stroked her neck again.

When I went back down to the living room, it occurred to me I wasn't going to be able just to walk right out of the house.

In fact, I had to wait almost two hours before Mrs. Pinchon opened the kitchen door again.

Spent the time eating leftovers from all the cats' food dishes.

When the door finally opened, I dashed outside between Mrs. Pinchon's ankles.

"Oh, my God!" she cried in exasperation. "What in the world were *you* doing in here?"

All the way home I thought of the aging cat in the upstairs basket. She seemed to hold the secrets of a happy life in her dark, speckled eyes.

I hope when my time comes, I can go like that.

Mrs. Axe fell over Bobbie Boop this morning. She was rushing through the house with a broom and dustpan. She didn't see him sleeping in the middle of the rug.

When she pulled herself up, she looked at him with such a steely expression of loathing I thought she was going to hit him over the head with the broom.

Mrs. Axe was on the phone bright and early this morning. She called the newspaper.

"I want to place a want ad," she said. "Yes, I'll hold."

She tapped her fingers hard on the phone stand and hummed a military march.

"Yes, I'd like to place an ad. 'Cats—free to good home.' No, I don't want to describe the cats. What's to describe? A cat's a cat . . . How should I know how old they are? No, that's all I want to say. When will that run? Good. The sooner the better."

She hung up the phone.

Mrs. Axe began a thorough housecleaning today. She started with the living room.

She yanked an armchair away from the living-room wall. She stared down behind it in disbelief.

"What is *this*?!" she muttered.

She'd found Bobbie Boop's secret stash of favorite things.

There were Mrs. V's reading glasses, the toaster, half a dozen pieces of paper money, numerous pieces of cellophane, a long red string, a Ping-Pong ball, three Christmas ornaments, a turkey bone, two wadded-up napkins, and a roll of Christmas ribbon.

"Poor, poor thing," Mrs. Axe mumbled. "Imagine stuffing your glasses behind an old chair!"

She pulled everything out and threw it away except for the money, the glasses, and the toaster.

"It's a good thing I'm here to take care of her," said Mrs. Axe as she dumped it all in the trash. "I just hope if I ever get that dotty, someone will have the kindness to put me out of my misery."

Strangers at the front door this morning. A man and a woman in their thirties. They had a little girl with them.

"Oh, Mommy, he's adorable!" said the girl rushing up to Bobbie Boop.

Bobbie Boop blinked at her in confusion.

"Can we, can we, can we?" said the girl.

"I'm just not sure," said the woman. She sighed.

"I still say we need a *dog*," said the man. He looked irritated. "What's the use of a cat anyway?"

"Oh, please, please, please, please, please," begged the girl.

"Take him," said Mrs. Axe.

In an instant Bobbie Boop was gone. I sat in the front window and watched as he was carried away and felt as if my heart were going to burst.

"We'll never find a home for you," Mrs. Axe told Zachary. "It's the pound for you tomorrow."

Zachary disappeared this morning. Mrs. Axe looked everywhere for him. "Here, kitty-kitty," she called ever so sweetly. "Come out and face the music . . ." She had the carrying case open on the dining-room table.

She grew edgy when she couldn't find him.

"Come on out, kitty-kitty," she tried again. "Be a good little kitty and take your medicine like a man."

She stood in the middle of the dining room with her hands on her hips.

"It's no use," she finally hollered in a firm voice. "You can't hide. I'll find you eventually."

She spent two hours looking for him. She never found him.

She was so annoyed that when she went to put the carrying case away, she looked at me as if she were going to throw *me* in it, just to have something to take to the pound.

A middle-aged couple came to the door this evening.

"This the cat?" asked the man, pointing at me.

"He's yours if you want him," said Mrs. Axe.

"What do you think?" the man asked his wife.

She made a face. "You don't have something in peach or taupe, do you?" she asked Mrs. Axe.

"This is it," said Mrs. Axe. "Take him or leave him."

"He wouldn't go with the furniture," said the wife.

They left.

The Christmas tree was gone this morning. There was no explanation. Mrs. Axe was mumbling to herself about "stupid, sentimental people" as she cleaned up fallen pine needles and pieces of broken Christmas ornaments from around the corner of the living room where the tree had stood.

A couple in their forties came to the door this afternoon.

The man stared at me unhappily. "He looks old," he grumbled.

"I have to have a kitten," said the woman. "I don't need anything else to remind me how old I'm getting. We agreed. It has to be a kitten. I want something to make me feel young again."

They walked out.

"Does he have papers?" another woman inquired an hour later. "We were hoping you were giving purebreds away."

"I need a cat to help train my bull terrier for dog fights," said a man who came after that.

Mrs. Axe looked tempted, but she refused.

"Oh, it's a *cat*," said a woman half an hour later. She giggled. "I must've misread the ad. I thought you were giving away *cars*." She couldn't stop giggling as she left.

The doorbell rang again late this evening. It was Mrs. Thornhill.

"I want to speak to you," she told Mrs. Axe.

"What about?"

"You're giving Mrs. Vigil's cats away," said Mrs. T.

"That's right."

"Did she ask you to?"

"She's in no condition to be making any decisions," said Mrs. Axe. "I nearly broke my neck over one of them a few days ago. You think a woman in her condition should be coming home to that?"

"Is this the only one left?" asked Mrs. T. She pointed at me.

"Yep."

"I'll take him."

"What do you mean?"

"I want him. I'll take him home with me. Now."

"You sure?"

Mrs. T glared at her.

Mrs. Axe handed me over. "He's yours," she said.

Christmas Eve. Spent the day locked in one of Mrs. T's upstairs bedrooms.

"You have to stay in here for now," she told me, "until I get the dog accustomed to you."

She brought me a bowl of food, a bowl of water, and a litter box. It wasn't the kind of food I'm used to, but I didn't make an issue of it.

When she left, she accidentally left the door ajar. I pulled it open with my claws. Dashed out to explore the house. Was just about to go downstairs when the "dog" suddenly appeared.

He glowered at me angrily and slowly opened his mouth. I could see nothing but two seemingly endless rows of razor-sharp teeth. He arched his back as if he was going to attack, and all the hair went up along his spine. Saliva was dripping from his teeth.

I raced back into the bedroom and hid under the bed.

Early this evening, I was looking out the back window. For a moment I thought I saw Zachary on Mrs. Thornhill's back fence. But then he disappeared.

Don't go home, I thought to myself. Whatever you do, Zachary, don't go home . . .

Could hear everyone singing Christmas carols downstairs tonight. Lots of laughter, the sound of presents being opened.

"Oh, I love it!" I heard Mrs. T's daughter exclaim. "Oh, Mother—it's beautiful!"

Slept.

Dreamt of Bobbie Boop and Mrs. V.

Mrs. T let me out to spend Christmas Day downstairs. The dog was in the backyard. I slept by the fire most of the day. Couldn't even get up enough enthusiasm to knock a couple of ornaments off the Christmas tree.

Overheard Mrs. T and her daughter talking in the kitchen.

"He *can't* stay here," said the daughter. "The dog'll get him."

"I told you," Mrs. T said with a sigh. "He isn't *going* to stay here. As soon as Mrs. Vigil's home and Mrs. Axe leaves, I'll take him back. The problem is, how to get rid of Mrs. Axe."

Sat in the kitchen window looking out back this afternoon.

Saw Mrs. Axe suddenly peek over the fence into Mrs. T's backyard.

The "dog" spotted her and growled at her angrily.

Mrs. Axe didn't blink. She didn't move. She glared at him contemptuously.

"You don't scare me," I could hear her tell him. "Where I come from we *know* how to deal with your kind!"

He charged the fence.

"Think you're pretty tough, don't you?" said Mrs. Axe. "Dog, indeed!" she hissed. "People here are so stupid they don't even know what they have living in their own backyards!"

All the hair on Vlad's back was sticking up so straight he looked like a hyena. A thick froth was pouring from his mouth.

"In Montana, we'd skin you alive and hang you over the fireplace!" Mrs. Axe taunted him.

He charged the fence again. The fence bent a little from the impact.

"Go on," Mrs. Axe told him. "Go ahead. Come and get me. Stupid creature. If I had a gun, I'd shoot you!"

She disappeared.

Vlad stood in the middle of the yard. He was panting. His eyes were on fire.

He growled for a moment, then sat down and started gnawing a hole in the fence.

Mrs. Thornhill and her daughter went out for dinner tonight.

I was locked up in the guest room again.

Light snow today. Sat thinking of the time Bobbie Boop went racing from window to window trying to catch snowflakes. Thought of the time Mrs. V found him sleeping in the soup pot and told him, "An idle Boop is the Devil's workshop." Thought of the time the four of us baked Christmas cookies.

Mrs. T came into the guest room late this morning.

"Your mother's coming home today," she announced.

She didn't seem happy.

"I don't think you should go home yet," she added. "There are problems."

I sat in a front window all afternoon and watched for some sign of Mrs. V.

In late afternoon, a car finally pulled up in front of her house.

Mrs. Axe got out of the passenger side. Mrs. T got out of the driver's seat.

They opened the trunk and pulled out a wheelchair.

Then they opened one of the back doors and helped a frail, very skinny woman into the chair.

The woman's head slumped to one side. Her left arm was shaking uncontrollably.

It was Mrs. V.

They wheeled her into the house.

"Why don't you go outside for a little while to-day?" Mrs. Thornhill told me this morning. "The dog's in the garage . . ."

It was good to see sunlight again.

Once outside, I hopped over the fence into Mrs. V's backyard. Jumped from window to window of the house looking for her. There was no sign of her in the kitchen. No sign of her in her study.

Finally I jumped up and looked through the bedroom window. I could see Mrs. V lying in bed.

Pawed at the screen to get her attention.

She didn't respond.

Pawed at the screen again.

Mrs. Axe came into the bedroom carrying a food tray.

She spotted me.

She set down the tray and rushed to the window and opened it.

"Get out of here!" she commanded. "Out! Go away! This isn't your home anymore! Get away from here!"

She banged on the screen to scare me.

Mrs. V moaned from her bed.

"Get away right now, or I'll come out there and *throw* you over the fence!"

Mrs. V moaned again.

"Can't you see *you* did this?!" Mrs. Axe snapped at me, slamming the window shut.

I sat in the window a moment longer. Felt stunned.

Went back to Mrs. T's yard.

Sat in the grass a long time.

Out in the backyard again today. Cold but sunny. Mr. Bull came over, and we chased each other around the lilacs for a while. Slept in the sunshine after that. Stayed away from Mrs. V's yard.

Mrs. T took me inside in the late afternoon so she could let the dog out.

I sat in a kitchen window, looking out back. Nice sunshine coming in. It felt warm and soothing.

Was dozing off when I saw Mrs. Axe suddenly appear from behind her side of the back fence. She surveyed the yard. An ugly smile crossed her face when she spotted Vlad.

The moment he saw her, he started growling. He didn't move at first. He lay with his head on his front paws. He glared at her and growled.

Mrs. Axe pulled a thick, raw steak up into view from behind the fence.

"Come and get it, bozo," she snarled.

Every muscle in Vlad's body went on alert.

He snorted. He hunched his back. He pulled his front paws in close to his body.

Then he moved so fast it was like a blur across

the yard. He leapt over the grass and jumped at the steak. At the very moment he might've closed his jaws around it, Mrs. Axe pulled a shovel into view with her other hand and hit him on the head with it.

She laughed.

"Stupid animal," she hissed.

He fell to the ground and then instantly leapt at the steak again.

Mrs. Axe hit him in the head, hard, with the shovel again.

She laughed.

He leapt again, not at the steak this time but at her.

The fence started to bend under the impact of his body.

"Big and powerful and stupid," Mrs. Axe taunted him.

"Come on," she snarled. "Come and get me."

The fence bent even more under a second impact.

"Next time it won't be a shovel," she threatened. "It'll be a gun!"

She disappeared.

He stood in the yard staring at the fence with such a terrible hatred I thought he would plow a hole right through it.

Instead, he turned and grabbed one of Mrs. T's big rosebushes with his teeth. He yanked and yanked until he pulled the entire bush out of the ground. Then he started ripping it to pieces.

Terrible noises in the backyard last night. A loud bang, growling, and then a grinding noise. Another loud bang, then screaming and an awful, low whimper. There was a sound like a cat food can being opened after that.

I leapt into a back window. It was too dark to see anything.

Mrs. T rushed to the door.

"Vlad!" she shouted. "Vlad, come in!"

There was no sign of him.

"Vlad!" she shouted again. "It's time to come in now."

She waited. Nothing.

She grabbed a flashlight and went out to look for him.

She was gone a very long time.

"Oh, Vlad . . . Oh, Vlad . . ." I heard her exclaim mournfully in the darkness.

When she came back in, her hands were covered with dirt.

I thought Vlad must be dead, but later I heard him baying, rather happily it seemed to me, at the moon.

Mrs. Axe has disappeared. No one knows where she is.

"It's the strangest thing I've ever seen," Mrs. T told me this morning when she came to get me out of the guest room. She seemed very cheerful. "No note, no message, nothing. She left everything behind."

Mrs. T picked me up and held me in her arms.

"I suppose we'll have to call the police sometime," she told me. "But for now, *you're* going home."

She kissed me on the top of the head.

Then she held me for a moment staring into my eyes.

"What exactly did you see last night from the window, I wonder," she said.

There were suddenly tears in her eyes.

"Oh, I'm going to miss you," she said.

She sighed and carried me over to Mrs. V's house.

Mrs. V was sitting on the living-room sofa. She looked frail and old. She reminded me for a moment of the old cat I'd seen at the Pinchons'

house. She was dressed in her big, red kimono. Her head no longer slumped to one side, but she looked exhausted.

When she saw me, her eyes opened wide and started to fill with tears.

She tried to hold out her arms for me.

A big hug and a long kiss on the back of the neck followed.

"Pan . . ." she suddenly said with obvious difficulty. "Panda . . . pan-da . . ."

"No, darling," said Mrs. T. "This is a cat, not a panda."

She sighed sadly.

Mrs. V kept me on her lap all afternoon. "Panda . . ." she whispered again, stroking me on the head.

Mrs. T stayed with us all day.

In the evening, a strange car drove up. Mrs. T went to the door.

"Oh, thank God," I heard her say. "I can't thank you enough. You have no idea how much this means . . ."

"If we'd known," said a strange man, "we never would've taken him."

"Oh, it doesn't matter," said Mrs. T. "Thank you, thank you . . ."

"I'm just . . . real sorry," said the man.

Mrs. T shut the door.

I could hear the man telling someone outside, "I *told* you we should've gotten a dog." Mrs. T came into the living room. Bobbie Boop was in her arms.

The moment he saw Mrs. V, he squirmed loose and leapt through the air to the sofa and landed right next to her on the cushion and then rubbed himself ecstatically against the sleeve of her kimono.

Mrs. V kissed him and petted him and rubbed her cheek against his. Her hands were shaking.

"Panda," she started to gasp again. "Panda . . . panda . . ."

"No, no," said Mrs. Thornhill gently. "It's a *cat*, dear, not a panda . . ."

Mrs. V held Bobbie Boop and me on her lap.

I leaned over and licked Bobbie Boop's face. He licked me back.

We started licking each other's paws and ears and necks.

"If only I could figure out what happened to the third one, Zachary," said Mrs. T unhappily. She sighed. "I've looked everywhere for him."

"Panda," Mrs. V whispered haltingly. "Panda..."

"Yes, dear," Mrs. T finally told her distractedly. "It's a panda."

Got up bright and early. Chased a few dust balls around the dining room.

Went in to the kitchen to help Mrs. Thornhill's daughter fix coffee. She's staying with us for a while to help Mrs. V.

No sign of Mrs. Axe.

No sign of Zachary. He had disappeared as mysteriously as he had first come here.

Bobbie Boop and I wrestled on the living-room floor for a few minutes. Then we joined Mrs. V on her bed.

Mrs. T's daughter came in with the coffee.

Mrs. V nodded at her, and a strange sound came up from her throat.

"You're welcome," said Mrs. T's daughter.

Mrs. T came over later to read to Mrs. V.

Mrs. Ridgeway came over after that with some freshly baked pie and cookies.

And Mr. Butler and Mr. Fielding came over in the evening to tell Mrs. V all about Mr. Fielding's latest trip.

Went to sleep feeling very content. Bobbie Boop and I slept on Mrs. V's pillow with our paws all mixed up in her hair.

Was outside today. Played in the backyard.

Jumped up on the fence. Mrs. T's "dog" was chained up in her yard. He glanced at me indifferently.

Mrs. T came out with a bowl of food for him. She didn't see me.

She set it down next to him, then gently stroked his head. He gave her hand an affectionate lick.

"My beautiful little . . ." She looked at him questioningly. "What are you anyway?" she asked. She smiled. "My beautiful little Vlad." She sighed. "I don't blame you for what happened," she told him. "It was self-defense . . ." She went inside.

I suddenly noticed something strange down in the dirt of one of the flower beds. It looked like a small piece of fabric.

Jumped off the fence to examine it.

Vlad growled at me, but I don't think he meant anything by it.

I dug around in the flower bed a little. Pulled out a small piece of cloth. It looked like part of a dress.

It smelled of chlorine bleach.

Then I noticed Mrs. V's shovel—the one Mrs. Axe had used to hit Vlad—leaning up in a corner of Mrs. T's yard.

Played in Mrs. V's closet this morning. Bobbie Boop and I chased each other around the boxes and in between the coats and dresses. We accidentally brought down an entire shelf of old shoes.

"No! No!" Mrs. T's daughter hollered. "Out of there! Out of there! Right now!"

She picked up Bobbie Boop and tossed him on the bed. She swatted me out from a corner of the closet.

"You two clowns go play somewhere else," she told us.

I jumped on the bed.

Mrs. V was smiling at me and Bobbie Boop.

She reached for both of us and held us close.

Mrs. Thornhill's daughter picked up shoes from all over the floor.

"Panda..." Mrs. V suddenly said. "Panda..."

I could suddenly feel a little more strength in her fingers.

"Panda ..." she said.

She was struggling with the word.

"Panda ... mo ... pande ... mo ... nee ... um," she said.

I looked up at her face.

Tears were coming down her cheeks.

"Pandemonium," she said, "thy . . . name . . . is . . . cat."

SPRING

Slept.

March 5

Slept.

Food fight with Bobbie Boop this morning. I don't even remember what started it, but by the time Mrs. V came into the kitchen, we had overturned the water dishes and the food bowls, and there was dry cat food all over the kitchen floor.

Bobbie Boop continued batting the food around even while Mrs. V got down on the floor and tried to pick it up.

"If you weren't so . . . cute," she told him haltingly, "I'd have you turned into an Easter bonnet . . ."

That seemed to sober him up. He sat looking at her mortified, his eyes wide open, with an expression that immediately moved her to guilt.

"Oh, I'm *sorry*," she said. She picked him up and hugged him for several minutes. "I shouldn't even . . . joke . . ."

When you're cute, you can get away with almost anything.

Lay in the grass. Chased a fly. The fly wound up on top of the mailbox, and so did I. I was perched there trying to keep my balance, when the same two women who last summer had been discussing what cats think about strolled by.

"If I ever get a pet," said the one, looking askance at me, "it will certainly be a dog."

"Why do you say that?" asked the other.

"Have you ever walked down the street and seen a *dog* on top of a mailbox?"

"Of course not," said the other.

"I rest my case. Cats have no sense."

"My Persian, Sweetpea, has sense," the other protested. "She has more sense than most people I know . . ."

I toppled off the mailbox.

"See?" said the one. "No sense at all. Dogs know their place. But a cat will embarrass you every time."

Prowled around the neighborhood after that. It smelled like spring in every yard.

Trotted down to Mr. Butler's garden. He was digging in the dirt. His daffodils and crocuses have started coming up.

I rolled in his flower bed. The dirt felt warm and soft.

He laughed.

"You think it smells good now," he said. "Just wait till I add manure . . ."

Mr. Fielding brought out a glass of iced tea for him and smiled at me.

Mrs. Pinchon was up in a tree in front of her house. She was clutching a limb with one hand while holding out an open can of cat food to a terrified stray about two feet above her.

"Mmm, mmm," she murmured. "There's more where that came from. Mmm—catnip, too."

The stray hissed at her but leaned forward, full of curiosity and hunger.

Mrs. Ridgeway was out fertilizing her front lawn.

Bobbie Boop and Brigitte were curled up together on her front porch, enjoying the sunshine.

Mrs. Ridgeway smiled and waved to me as I trotted by.

I sat for a long time in Mrs. Thornhill's front yard. Watched a couple of bugs. Saw the first grasshopper of the season. Felt too content to chase him. There'll be plenty more where he came from.

Mrs. Thornhill's daughter and her boyfriend came out the front door. They were both dressed in torn jeans and dirty T-shirts.

"Don't forget laundry detergent," Mrs. T hollered from the door.

"Yeah, yeah," her daughter replied indifferently.

I looked up at Mrs. T standing in the doorway.

She gazed at me a long time and then smiled.

"Sometimes," she said, "there's nothing to do but embrace the inevitable." She gave me a little laugh. "But you know that. You're a cat . . ."

She closed the door.

Walked the fences for a while.

Was on the fence between Mrs. V's yard and the Gowers' behind us, when I suddenly heard the Whittlesee boy calling out, "Ted-dy! Ted-dy!" from his backyard.

I've heard him call that name several times in the last few weeks.

"Ted-dy!" he called again. "Where are you, Teddy?"

A flock of geese flew overhead. They were going north. The sight of them made me sigh.

"Oh, there you are!" I overheard the Whittlesee boy say. "Why did you run off like that, Teddy? It's time for lunch now."

I wandered over to see who he was talking to.

"Oh, Teddy," I heard him say. "It's almost summer again."

I looked down into the yard.

The Whittlesee boy was sitting on the grass eating a sandwich. A cat was sitting on his lap. Every so often, the boy pulled off a piece of lunch meat and fed it to the cat.

"We're going to have a wonderful summer, aren't we, Teddy?" the boy told the cat. "We're going to climb trees together and explore the neighborhood. And every night we'll curl up together in my sleeping bag, and we'll sleep with the moon in our faces . . ."

He gave the cat a big hug.

"We're buddies, aren't we, Teddy?" he said. "I'm so glad you came into my life . . ."

It took me a moment to realize what I was seeing. The cat was Zachary. Plump and healthy and happy. His legs were no longer like twigs, and he no longer had a forelorn, searching look in his eyes. He sat in the boy's lap and ate the little pieces of lunch meat, and then rubbed his head with ardent affection against the boy's arm. The boy, too, seemed less pale, less unhappy.

Zachary suddenly leaned over and nibbled the boy's nose affectionately.

The Whittlesee boy giggled.

"Oh, Teddy," he whispered. "I'll love you forever."

About the Author

LEIGH W. RUTLEDGE recently moved himself and his twenty-four cats from the mountains of Colorado to the sands of Key West, Florida. He is the author of, among other books, *A Cat's Little Instruction Book*, *Cat Love Letters*, and *Dear Tabby*.